G000126345

Codesigning
Space_____ a primer

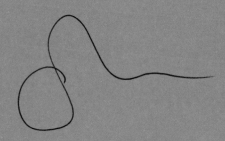

TILT®

Artifice
books on architecture

Theory _____ 12

Practice _____ 56

Appendix _____ 134

Codesigning Space _____

Foreword

Codesign has a venerable history, going back hundreds of years—and long before the very modern distinction between the professionals who design buildings and the people who use them.

The last great explosion of codesign was in the 1970s and 1980s, a time of community architecture and the humanist approach of pioneers such as Ralph Erksine. Codesign has dipped in and out of fashion since, but has re-emerged over the last three years to become a significant force once more.

The current recession is a powerful catalyst for innovation; for finding new and more cost-effective ways of getting things done, including cutting out the middleman. Putting users and designers in direct contact has created a more immediate and democratic dialogue which itself has gained momentum. There has been a cultural shift by which a new generation of practitioners has begun to question the way that things have been built over the last 20 years or so, and a renewed interest in the process of design itself—politically, economically and socially.

I sense a deep disillusionment about the prevailing conditions that have created a generation of Starchitects and a portfolio of iconic buildings that serve only a few. Many of our cities are in near terminal decline, or transformation, leading to critiques of the so-called Bilbao Effect—a sometimes superficial combination of iconic architecture and new consumerism—as a universal solution for regeneration.

Throw into the mix the changing role itself of the architect—currently under severe pressure from profit-driven contractors and private developers who are dominating the process by which things get made, and replacing the State as the dominant client of the last 40 years—and you have a perfect storm for the re-emergence of codesign.

Instead of allowing themselves to be marginalised, designers and architects are re-thinking their role to find new models of practice more akin to activism.

TILT is one of a number of organisations operating at this intersection, combining activism with entrepreneurial activity. In this stimulating book, TILT explore the changing role of designers at this very particular moment in time. Operating between public and private, crisis and utopia, the studio is attempting to define a new approach which does not so much respond to a given brief, but tries instead to actively create the conditions under which buildings and spaces can be created.

Clearly, crisis conditions are creating a fertile bed for innovation, with IT and communications enabling a new, more democratically driven, culture to emerge. In design, as in other areas, there is a kind of democratisation of control over factors previously enjoyed only by the establishment.

The question now is do we find a new role for the State in directing the process of design and the conditions by which it operates, or do we find new ways to connect the private and public sectors? Can codesign coexist alongside an imperfect system, or does it require a more radical shift, of the kind TILT talk about in this book, to gain proper traction in society as the preferred methodology for getting things done.

It's a bit wild west out there, and it would take a brave individual to predict which way things will go, but for now this is an exciting time to be a pioneer.

Manifesto for a young practice.
Principles for codesign.

1. Engage the end-user in the process. The designing process must transform people's relationship with space and the making of space. 2. Design is in the hands of the many, not the few. Bringing diverse perspectives into a process leads to a better outcome. 3. The role of the designer and architect is evolving. Codesign prevents both designer and client from designing only in their own interest. 4. Scepticism can offer a hidden perspective. Listening to voices of doubt and dissent can open new perspectives and offer a chance to challenge accepted wisdom. 5. Pluralism over unity. Consensus shouldn't guide design, instead critical deliberation should inform a better choice. 6. Challenge one-dimensionality. Designers should be facilitators and enable a community to acknowledge individuals and their latent talents. 7. Codesign offers a chance for a civic

education. Everyone is learning through this process. 8. There's a sense of purpose around everything. Don't get detached from what design is supposed to do–enable people to improve their lives. 9. Make it locally and make it out of the right material. Designers and end-users should be connected with making and respect what it is. 10. Don't design products for products' sake. Creating meaningful design with users is a sustainable design model. 11. Tension is an asset. Trust complexity and emergence as something that will be effective in solving a problem. Engaging people in a shared design process is always more effort than designing alone but much more powerful. 12. Shift the design paradigm. Collaborative design and the engagement of end-users should be the norm, not the exception.

Theory

_____ **Dermot Egan**

Dermot Egan is Managing Director at TILT. Here he introduces the
practice, its genesis and motivations. He also gives an outline to the
critical elements of TILT's approach and some of the challenges faced
in its short history.

All men and women are designers

We have constructed a boundary between creative people
and everyone else. Nowhere has this been more evident
than in the design and delivery of our built environment.
In the field of architecture and spatial design, the intuition
and intent of the designer has routinely taken precedent
over the needs of the end-user, almost entirely eradicating
meaningful dialogue in the process. The result has been
a huge number of spaces in both the private and public
sphere that fail to serve their purpose—designed for a
fictitious set of users. Offices that make people tired and
unmotivated to work, hospital waiting rooms that make
patients and visitors feel ill, ineffectual job centres and so
on. Not all the blame for this can be placed on the vanity
of designers, however, as clients and developers also play
their part. Whichever way we view it, something needs to
be done to end this vicious cycle.

Within this context, the vision for TILT's practice is
simple: to demystify architecture and design and deliver
refreshing spaces that better complement the purpose
and personality of the people that use them. To achieve
this, TILT has been implementing a codesign methodology
that actively engages the users of a space in all stages

of the design process, from the initial briefing to making
the space. This process encourages users to explore the
role of objects, furniture and design in their space, and
its impact on their own culture and behaviour. As Victor
Papanek said in *Design for the Real World* (1974) more
than 40 years ago: "All men and women are designers.
All that we do almost all the time is design, for design is
basic to all human activity."

At the heart of TILT's codesign approach is the fundamental
logic that developing the design of a space through
participation with those who will ultimately use it makes
practical sense. Like anything that centres on human
actions and experience, there is an emotional component,
a transformational effect that this approach can have,
which leads to spaces that have more impact and that
help strengthen communities. Through this process, the
space develops a purposeful narrative that is shaped and
evolved by its users.

Codesign is not a new concept. While TILT's work builds
on ideas that have been established for decades, our
contribution to codesign is to develop a coherent process

for designing spaces collaboratively that enables a designer to take participants on a journey with a tangible result. While challenging the traditional role of the designer, TILT still respects the role of the professional designer, who can deliver all the conventional elements crucial to the success of any building project while simultaneously holding the intentions of the community. However, it is our belief that this role needs to evolve to reflect the facilitative skills required to deliver codesigned spaces effectively.

Throughout this book we have expanded the discussion of codesign beyond TILT's own practice to encompass views from an eclectic range of individuals who offer a perspective on our ideas. Through their contributions, we wish to place this book where we believe it belongs, in the context of a much wider movement for a paradigm shift in design thinking and practice.

So this book is a primer to our way of codesigning spaces and is by no means exhaustive or comprehensive. We are sharing our experiences as a practice at a moment in time and through the lens of our codesign activities all connected to our project work. It is an ever-evolving methodology, developing as our practice grows and learns.

Our hope is that through this book we can inspire some and connect with others who share the same commitment to codesigning spaces. We would love to see this book as part of a growing knowledge base, so together we can fundamentally shift the practice of architecture and space design.

Codesigning Space

This graphic represents TILT's codesign process in its entirety. It contains many stages that will be familiar to the architect/designer, which are required to complete any building project successfully. The key distinction is the codesign activities that exist throughout each phase of the project and our commitment to embedding the principles of codesign in the process.

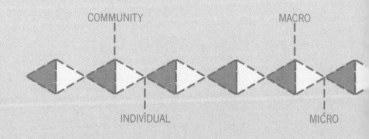

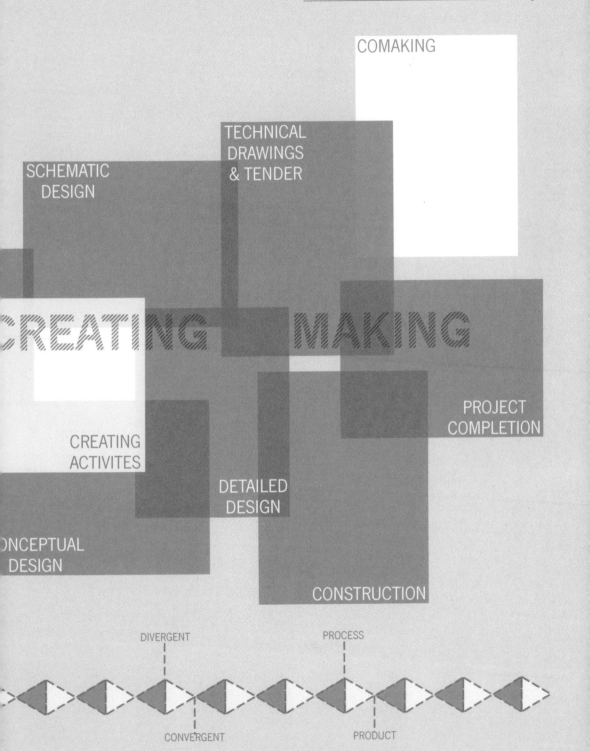

COMAKING

TECHNICAL
DRAWINGS
& TENDER

SCHEMATIC
DESIGN

CREATING MAKING

PROJECT
COMPLETION

CREATING
ACTIVITES

DETAILED
DESIGN

CONCEPTUAL
DESIGN

CONSTRUCTION

DIVERGENT

PROCESS

CONVERGENT

PRODUCT

David Lan is Artistic Director of the Young Vic Theatre in London. In his rich and extensive working life, Lan has been a filmmaker, a director and an anthropologist. Lan's enthusiasm and advocacy led to the rebuilding of the theatre in 2006 by architects Haworth Tompkins, which went on to win various awards, and was shortlisted for the Stirling Prize. Here, Oliver Marlow, who was on the design team for the redesign, interviews Lan.

The thing you make and the way it's received

OM   Can you speak to the idea of community, and about how theatre fosters a collective creativity?

DL   What is a community? It's a difficult word and used in so many different ways and often used, not deliberately malevolently, as a means to conceal rifts and antagonism. A community needs to see itself as a community before it can function as one. It leads to all kinds of difficulties knowing who you are and knowing what you want and when you've achieved it. The thing I'm dealing with all the time is ego, or individual people trying to make their way in the big world and the smaller worlds that people occupy. The positive side is potential—what's the point of this place? It's for the largest number of people to fulfil themselves as artists or just as people. You bring them together and the point is that they get something out of that experience, which is helpful in terms of becoming themselves. That's the wonderful side of ego.

The difficulty is when the individual can't quite find their place in a group and doesn't have a good understanding of what their contribution could be or needs to be and so you go swerving all over the place. A lot of what I try to do is create an environment in which the different egos can work together. The thing we need to have here is a sense of what it is we're trying to achieve and if that is strongly enough expressed then what we're trying to do is not for us, it's for them. It's not what we're trying to do in this building, it's what what we're doing in this building achieves for other people. Provided you can keep that focus, however it's placed—it's on the artists, the young people, the audience, but it's not about us.

OM   Do you think authenticity comes from a clear direction that everyone can
      be a part of, so they know that if they express themselves within it it will be
      valid and valuable?

DL   In a theatre, it is the quality of the work. It has to be good. What makes something
      authentic? Feeling, I suppose. The way I try to understand it is that the job is to
      create experience. What we're doing here is talking—it's a conversation. We're
      talking in a particular way. The thing about art is it's concentrated: you speed
      things up or slow things down, which gives it a different quality from normal
      experience. It's intensified. What I'm after is what happens between the thing you
      make and the way it's received. That's an experience.

      If the experience is perceived to be authentic, you're in with a chance. The
      thing I like is if there's something happening on stage that seems authentic and
      of a high quality in terms of the intensity of the experience—which is a lot of
      information in the broadest sense, that's been communicated through thought
      and emotion. If that's going on to an audience that itself is complex—it's young,
      old, ethnically mixed—if there's real transmission going on, and you can see
      it; it's like wind in a field of wheat—you can read what's happening in people's
      minds. Then that is authenticity.

OM   Creating experience seems to be key. I like this idea that if you focus too
      much on the thing itself, the work, whatever that may be, and forget about
      the massive amounts of complexity and transmission that you can't control,
      you lose something.

      One of the things you have talked about in the past is that, whether we like
      it or not, we're forced into interpreting what we see and feel. In a theatrical
      space you've activated that space and are purposefully referencing
      that relationship. To me, that is the idea of positive tension, and it has
      resonance in architecture too. Are there particular elements to that tension
      that are crucial?

DL   None of the things you're talking about exist objectively. The space doesn't exist
      at all until there are people in it. Everything is constructed intellectually through
      the mind, through the brain, through perception, through the body. An amazing
      thing happens when you learn to drive; you learn to expand your body so that your
      skin and the epidermis of the body is the same thing and when you drive through
      a narrow gap, you're feeling the outside of the car with your skin. It's a miracle
      in that people can negotiate the tiniest movements; it's visual but the number
      of messages you're receiving and sending out are too many to analyse. There's
      something like that happening all the time. You walk into a room and there's a
      relationship between your body, the room and the walls and the roof—you're
      aligning yourself. What's going on in the space in a theatre is so complex. In
      our big room you and Haworth Tompkins created surfaces and shapes, and the
      relationships of objects to each other, in a way that was fluid. There are no hard
      edges, everything can turn into everything else—it's constantly capable of being
      reimagined, in a way that people aren't really conscious of. It creates a potential

for exchange and change. So, back to first principles, and it's paradoxical—one knows that the relationship between the body in which one lives permanently and spaces into which one temporarily goes are endlessly poetic, and one knows that because one can think about it objectively, but you can't live your life like that—you'd go mad. You have to learn to deal with it. The underground in the morning is really full and people are negotiating, it is a fantastic skill. Everyone's making a hundred thousand decisions about how you hold your body in a relationship with space and with one another each and every moment of the day. When you watch a play you're doing a version of what you do in life. You're receiving vast volumes of detailed information, which you're processing mostly unconsciously.

OM **We do various activities that enact or make real what you're talking about. It's fascinating when you take away the visual, for example, which is so immediate in terms of responses, and you're faced with negotiating space. Given what you are saying, is your role as facilitator helping to tell stories and suspend disbelief?**

DL At one level, what I'm looking for watching a show is the story, how it's being told. Each essential bit of the story—essential because to get to one bit you've got to go through something else, but that something else has to be in exactly the right place—can be told through colour, movement, light. You're trying to take control, and what's really enjoyable is when what you're trying to take control of is really complex. There are many elements and you're trying to align them all to make it coherent. So, speaking about community: the way I try to do what I do is create relationships with the people I work with, so that when I say it needs to be red not blue, they'll hear me and they won't see it as an instruction—somehow it's not my ego, it's about trying to achieve authenticity. It's also quite useful to say: "Take it out." If you challenge something, or challenge it in a radical way, it breaks and if you rupture assumptions by turning it upside down or saying it should be a dog not a cat, people will say: "No, it shouldn't be a dog, it should be a different-coloured cat." It's trying to move your way forward through guessing, feeling, responding. Trying to find the deep level that's common.

OM **Going back to what you said: in terms of intervening because it's about the work, it belongs to everyone you're engaging with instead of stepping forward and saying it should be like this. When you're having to turn emotions and feelings into actual things, it's this idea of the archaeology of decision-making. It's pretty much impossible to say why that was the case. But it is possible if you have a sense of where you are going. There's something about the inherent problematic of going from ideas and quick discussions and making it into a real thing that people can relate to. One designer, working with a group of people, said "I can't wait till all this arguing and talking is over and we can get to designing", and I thought that was the wrong way to look at it, because that is the work. You can't predict it ultimately, even if it's directed by a script—in theatre, for example—you still don't know.**

DL And that's profound.

Oliver Marlow

Oliver Marlow is Creative Director at TILT. Here he discusses his
motivations for designing using the workshop approach, bringing
people together for interaction, cross-pollination of ideas and
emergence.

The workshop as design setting

In the 1950s, American artist Allan Kaprow moved his work
out of the gallery setting and into the streets. Transitioning
from paintings to three-dimensional art and 'environments'
that could be rearranged by the audience, he further subverted
conventional art practice with the introduction of space,
time and public interaction in his influential 'Happenings'.
Inspired by this spatial participatory practice, and in line
with its philosophy that end-users are the primary agents of
change, TILT has appropriated the notion that actions and
interactions have a set of instructions, and that by providing
a context in which these can occur, and a set of activities to
stimulate these interactions between space, time and people,
such instructions can elicit the expectations, wishes and
requirements to inform an intuitive and responsive outcome.
In this way, the context becomes a stage on which to play out
these actions. In TILT's case this is the workshop setting—a
constructed environment from which a project's design brief
can be shaped by exploring existing narratives, building new
ones and investigating experiential qualities.

In setting up a place within which these Happenings could
take place, Kaprow and his colleagues sourced the props and
researched the site. Its limitations meant that sites could not
be reused and were considered spent. For TILT, space is part
of a complex system of continuous movements and shifts
in contexts, scenarios and uses. There is an ongoing motion
to everything, including our interactions and perceptions of
place and time, situated within process. To accept this chain
of thought is to understand space as interdependent with
people, the users. As American philosopher John Dewey
wrote: "The first great consideration is that life goes on in
an environment; not merely in it but because of it, through
interaction with it. No creature lives merely under its skin."
A user's engagement with the space affects the space and
it in turn changes, or influences the user. In this way, the
relationship can be considered symbiotic. "Until man enters
a building," said Brazilian architect Lina Bo Bardi, "climbs
the steps, and takes possession of the space in a 'human
adventure' that develops over time, architecture does not exist."

TILT's ambition lies in peeling the process back a stage
from Bo Bardi's perspective, so that the workshop
participants' emotions and physical responses—either to
an existing space or potential service—are the genesis
of design. Therefore, the "human adventure" begins
before the design is complete. Since the use of space

is more than the process behind its activation, there is a dimension of imagined, lived and perceived space that must also be mediated in the process. According to sociologist Henri Lefebvre, this "trialectic" characterises space as socially produced. Negotiating and facilitating this articulation through activities fosters exchanges between the participant, their perception of space and the tangible aspects of it. Engaging with a design process is therefore an experiential event. A workshop is, in many ways, an ideal setting for this to happen. Much like Kaprow's site-specific Happenings, the workshop represents a controlled blast zone, where parameters are drawn, activities carefully orchestrated, where the outcome is not predetermined.

Part of the concept behind hosting workshops as a stage for the codesign process is to critically recontextualise the space. In activating spaces as well as objects through a dialogue with end-users and by developing scenarios that facilitate different experiential activities, these spaces and objects become meaningful and effective. This context enables people to explore the materiality of space, its implicit characteristics, and interact with its physical features. Driven by emotive comprehension of our environments, there is an opportunity to build a narrative around what exists and what the space could be. Further to this idea of tacit space, there is no ontological foundation for the workshop setting, since the space discussed is in the imagination and the desires of the participants.

The workshop too implies a collective: a multiplicity of voices, of dialogue between subject and object, and useful productivity. Designing space collectively is not a new conceit. Since no space can be in isolation of a variety of users over its lifetime, anticipated and appropriated through a multitude of guises, it seems appropriate, if not obvious, that there should be a variety of hands working to shape that space. Indeed, various initiatives have placed the work back into the hands of the constituents. A workshop environment nurtures collective creativity, a generosity and an awareness and empathy for others who will share those spaces. It also eschews the common assumption that the final design is a single-authored monologue, something fetishised.

Making room for a degree of unpredictability and randomness is an important challenge of design. Part of this unpredictability is the inherent tensions within a collection of people. TILT's approach encourages this tension to be played out within the workshop context, so as to extract the dynamism and draw on the differences

that inevitably surface in trying to do something together. The inclusion and active participation of end-users has an immeasurable effect on a given environment. Similarly the impact of turning the user's gaze towards their direct environment, to look and feel their way around a space, is to activate it—and activating the imagination is a vital part of design. It is this connection with our senses that places us within a context; it facilitates comfort, belonging, confidence and spatial consciousness. This notion of sensory perception as a means of locating ourselves and providing a sense of cohesion over a place is explored in the phenomenological theories of Finnish architect Juhani Pallasmaa. In his essay "Hapticity and Time", he writes: "The architecture of the eye detaches and controls, whereas haptic architecture engages and unites. Tactile sensibility replaces distancing visual imagery by enhanced materiality, nearness and intimacy." It is nothing short of arrogance to assume that we, as designers, know better than what the person who will be left using that space or sitting in that chair needs, and that the stimulation from these is only in beholding them.

A community is itself a creative resource, bubbling with innate skillsets, sometimes explicit but oftentimes not. The onus is therefore on the designer to establish a context and employ appropriate props or tools to engage people as co-conspirators in transforming their own environment. In *The Production of Space* (1991), Lefebvre writes: "A social transformation, to be truly revolutionary in character, must manifest a creative capacity in its effects on daily life, on language and on space."

This approach to working with and among conditions both human and constructed, has been compartmentalised in architecture and design practice until fairly recently. Its resurgence—led by an increasing interest in ownership over placemaking and a renewed respect for intuitive design—is spilling over into multiple areas of work: from policy-making to community engagement and top-down systems. The workshop stems from an instinct for gathering and debating, the need for a productive relationship between interaction with a site, its materials and its narrative, to evolve meaningful design.

Irena Bauman

Irena Bauman is co-founder of Bauman Lyons Architects, based in Leeds. She is Professor of Sustainable Urbanism at Sheffield University School of Architecture and is the Chair of Yorkshire Design Review. Her learning from architecture's failings as much as its successes has been an inspiration for the improvement of placemaking and is an inspiration for TILT. In July, Bauman and Marlow interviewed one another. Out of this conversation, Bauman wrote this essay.

At best architecture is about placemaking

Architecture provides protected and controlled environments for human activities. It is an expression of cultural values, meaning and identity. At its best, architecture interfaces with its context to create man-made places that enhance our experience of being together.

Architecture, however splendid, does not itself create good places. Places are created by our activities. The essential ingredient of good placemaking is an aspiration for 'civicness' in architecture expressed generously to society. It is the offer of a physical fabric as a backdrop, containing and facilitating a wide variety of public activities.

Enhancing civicness through architectural design has been short on patronage as the dominant priorities of the last two decades have been more concerned with political gain, risk mitigation, profit, speed and, in many cases, the vanity of the wealthy. Furthermore, the benefits of good placemaking, though demonstrable, are complex to measure; our social and economic constructs of 'value' favour quantifiable outputs. Whilst we have evidence that good places tend to be economically robust, the absence of accurate metrics for this added value, as well as the extra effort such evidencing requires, are constant setbacks.

Globalisation means that those who build are often remote from the communities for which they are building; the impact of their architecture on placemaking interests them little as they sell on their asset. It is a process that separates the building of cities from civic responsibility.

The profit-driven developments of recent times were sparked off by the well-meaning 1999 Urban White Paper formulated by the Urban Task Force under the chairmanship of Lord Rogers. Encouraging an increase in density in the private sector of city centres, the paper inadvertently gave licence to the opportunistic private sector to build quickly, before the public sector had the chance to put planning strategies into place that could have channelled this considerable investment into good placemaking. In this process, devoid of civic ambitions, landowners appropriated exterior space as a commodity to be controlled and managed.

Instead of streets animated by a variety of spontaneous activities, we have malls patrolled by uniformed men with curly wires plugged into their ears and public squares run by councils as profit-making venues programmed to entertain paying audiences.

The question that architects might ask is whether we are prepared to take responsibility for our complicity in this poor placemaking. Architects have a critical role, despite being only the intermediary between those who commission buildings and those who pay for them. We have the skills and knowledge to understand the consequences of our designs. But few architects acknowledge the failures of their schemes, and fewer still decline to work on poor projects.

Just as architectural commissioning is driven by commercial return and, at times, by vanity, so is the architectural 'establishment'. We rarely question the civic content of our projects and rarely evaluate the impact of our work. Instead we publish our projects in a journal (for other architects) within a couple of weeks of completion, then submit them for an award or two to be granted a few months later (selected by a panel of architects). For the vast majority of mediocre projects we choose not to reflect at all on what we have built. In either process we studiously avoid opening ourselves to feedback from wider society and fail to discuss why it should be that, on the few occasions where an award allows for a 'people's choice', the choice is always different from that made by the professionals.

Over the last few years Bauman Lyons Architects has stopped submitting projects for awards and instead revisited finished projects and asked users and clients for formal feedback. The impact of this on the practice has been profound; it has made us question the very basis of architectural education and practice. The lessons from the feedback are multiple and diverse; in the context of this publication two related issues have come to light that pose the most immediate questions.

First the realisation that all architectural briefs are temporal in nature and that all buildings require modifications from the moment they are handed over to the users. There is a diverse range of reasons for this: lack of user consultation in both speculative and non-speculative projects; poor project management practice; poor design team skills; constantly changing economic, political, social and now environmental and technological context. The one certainty is that the building will need to continue to change. The dimension of time and evolution of form is not taught in schools of architecture and it is rare to find refurbishment and conservation studio projects. Architecture is mainly taught as a static object, an optimum snapshot in time that provides 'The Solution' to a given problem. The majority of student projects focus on new-build schemes with a single static brief.

We are now asking ourselves at the start of each design project what is the absolute minimum that has to be fixed within the design to provide the maximum that can be altered cheaply. Inevitably the answers lie in studying the typologies that have lasted best throughout the years: the adaptable Victorian warehouse, designed for strength, daylight and natural ventilation and the narrow-plan, concrete buildings of the 1960s being amongst the most robust examples.

The other lesson is the high price clients pay for the lack of prototyping in architecture to test what does and does not work before great amounts of money are invested in construction. It is inconceivable for cars and other products to reach users before they have been prototyped and tested. Architectural models are our answer to prototyping but, often presenting inaccurate information because of lack of realistic detail and context, they frequently do architecture a great injustice. They also distract from the need to test the actual workings of spaces and for future flexibility.

There is an ongoing project in Copenhagen that, for us, expresses the zeitgeist, representing new values in placemaking. In so doing, it exposes the outmoded nature of the profession's construct of award-worthy architecture.

On a major arterial road that crosses many neighbourhoods, the city of Copenhagen has been undertaking a closely monitored, staged process of testing, rebalancing the lane widths between cars, pedestrians and cycles. Every six months a little bit of highway width is taken away from the car and given to the bicycle—the effect is monitored before further reduction is made. The works are cheap and temporary and, when the permanent alterations are made, they will not only work, but have the support of thousands of users. This is resilient and sustainable placemaking.

These two lessons on the temporary nature of briefs and the lack of prototyping testify to the need for a different process of design and placemaking—one of stepping stones and small gestures, temporary fixes and 'meanwhile' uses, evaluation and modification, close collaboration and fewer ovations in favour of deeper understanding, humility and reflection.

Peter Head led the Planning and Integrated Urbanism Team at Arup from 2004–2011. His work overseeing the analysis and mapping of data through grassroots operations and cultural mining to improve living conditions in cities the world over is part of what he terms our Ecological Era. Here Marlow interviews Head.

Projects are no longer about creating just things

OM   **What are the essential ingredients in making large-scale projects work?**

PH   In the past, large-scale projects have been treated as delivering physical things, whereas I think most people now would agree that the creative process is one that should lead to delivering societal values through environmental, economic, social and other value propositions. Our starting point is where those values are clearly recognised so that the project financing, funding, procurement and delivery process is all about making sure those outcomes are secured and the project is loved and owned by everybody. At the moment, we don't have a good set of models and tools that relate the physical outcomes on large-scale projects to values of all kinds.

OM   **Do you think there's a critical point at which scale breaks down?**

PH   We've concluded that you can't really make transformational change unless you do it at a large scale and therefore I don't think [it will] happen by just designing LEED Platinum buildings for example. We need integrated systemic change to create circular economies and closed-loop systems. You cannot do that at a scale less than probably half a million people. The reason is as much about economics as anything; you can't get behavioural change and reorganisation of resource systems that make an impact unless you can get that number of people to work together collaboratively.

OM   Would this require legislation providing impetus and penalties, and big visions that ignite people's imagination?

PH   I think it's the latter particularly, and creating an environment in which you can innovate in every sense: in policy, technologies, governance structures, and so on. It's really a question of effectively removing centralised control and allowing a decentralised set of deliveries to happen within an overarching framework that's looking for certain outcomes. The problem is that, at the moment, no one understands a region of this scale completely. We need to create systems models to enable this understanding.

OM   Is it a question of aggregating small-scale processes, or is it possible to communicate with everyone for large-scale collaborations to be realised?

PH   We use a method called cultural planning, which is a way of engaging the cultural roots of people in the region and any group who may migrate there. You work through the cultural history, their relationship with communities, the land, the environment and physical things they've built. Through this process you find the cultural leaders, then you can work with them to find long-haul objectives. This can be done with a limited number of trusted people and [is] then discussed with their communities over a period of several months.

OM   If you're engaging these smaller groups, building up trust and a common vision, you can begin to show how that might look using modelling?

PH   Yes. We have local experts who start setting up the model, typically a college or university capable of using the open-source platform, and we ask those leaders and communities—including SMEs, government, people at home—to start populating the model with data so it is a representative here-and-now model of the region, which gives them all sorts of insights. Building this—through workshops, arts and cultural events—might take 10 months and produces a model that people own. Quite a lot of that data can come from global sources like earth observation satellites, but the social and economic data is crowd-sourced. The first outcome is a regional news stream. Then we set up a physical or virtual hub, or a combination, enabling people to collaboratively investigate changes and examine how everything can be improved.

OM   This idea of ownership seems key. Have you faced challenges in terms of people understanding how important it is to allow this free flow of information?

PH   We haven't got into that ourselves, but we work with people who have. One of the places doing this most progressively is Berlin, Germany. They're effectively crowd-sourcing an energy model for the city. People are flocking to do it because they're finding the data that comes back out again useful and interesting. Another example is in Africa and India where Slum Dweller's International is crowd-sourcing information in slums. The quality [of data] is very high because communities are gathering it themselves. You don't need to go through central or regional government, which is important to enable communities to make decisions for themselves.

OM Do you think it's a real seismic change or just something we're enabling with our technologies?

PH I think people generally sense the need to do things differently—we can't just go on as we are, but I don't think people quite know what it is that we ought to be doing, and that's very dispiriting. Taking this process through develops mutual respect and trust and when you have that, you can move forward much more quickly. In my view, that comes from being transparent and open, from listening and involving people rather than thinking up the solution and trying to persuade people to come on board, which is too much the norm.

OM Iteration, prototyping and testing things is standard in design disciplines other than architecture. Do you think we need to change how the built environment is presented or, because of the costs and scales, you have to go ahead and build big?

PH It comes back to the heart of what we call planning and design. It's about the user; it's the outcome for society that really matters. The creative process involves prototyping, testing and retesting but you can't do that unless you have a model [with] economic, social and environmental outcomes in it. For me, this is the game changer. There are diamond factories in Surat, Gujarat, which cut and polish 80 per cent of the world's small diamonds—each has 4,000 people using the highest technology, and I can't imagine why we aren't doing the same thing for the way people live in the cities. You've got to have a process that contains a continuous opportunity for creative people at different scales to collaborate and evolve the planning, design and delivery.

OM The idea is so simple it feels intuitive; it has its own momentum.

PH The difficulty is getting sufficient money up front for a development process to deliver this approach as a tool. A lot of people don't recognise that the procurement process is critical. [This approach] means that you still have competitive procurement of everything, but it's a design-and-build process that could be a public-private partnership, or not, and it's about procuring social/economic/environmental outcomes. It isn't about delivering the stuff.

OM How do you feel establishing these models is progressing and where do you think it's going?

PH I'm finding that there's a disconnect with [the] vision and the ability to deliver it. The solutions are not going to be delivered by big corporate players and the private sector. Regional governance is critical, and those countries that have a reasonably robust regional governance structure can do this more easily. This approach is going to be able to deliver faster capital for projects, because people want to deploy their capital into what they call 'good projects'. So there is a real opportunity here, which is to allow capital to be pulled into regions. There is a big appetite to do this but people still need to be persuaded to put cash on the table at the beginning of the journey.

_____ **Eileen Conn**

Eileen Conn has had a long-term interest in the dynamics of communities
and their interactions with public agencies and commercial companies.
She studies social dynamics and complex living systems, and works
for sustainable and cohesive communities. She was awarded an MBE
in 2009 for services to the community. Marlow interviews Conn about
community activism and systemic change.

Things are changing all the time

**OM   How do you think systemic change happens—is it through small
interventions that then proliferate or by top-down macro shifts?**

EC   If you have a macro intervention change will happen, but it's not necessarily the
change you're expecting. One thing that we're missing in our way of thinking is
that the systems we're trying to affect are living, organic, dynamic systems,
which are unpredictable, non-linear and unable to be manipulated perfectly.
We run everything like a machine, which is why it's not effective and why it has
perverse results. We're trying to devise all these policies and interventions without
understanding the distinction between the systems.

OM   What are the ways that you can influence or engage with these systems?

EC   There are two distinct systems interacting in a social ecosystems dance, and
their different dynamics have significant organisational effects. I call the systems
the 'vertical hierarchical' and the 'horizontal peer'. The dominant mode of the
vertical is of ordered authority and contractual relationships. In the horizontal
system, relationships are based on free and voluntary association, often called
the 'community'. These two systems interact in what complexity theory describes
as the 'space of possibilities', where evolution happens for organisms in their
interaction with their environment. It is a key place for influencing and engaging
with the systems. It is where change can happen. But the vertical system operates
as if the other system is just like itself and much of the interaction can therefore

be ineffectual or have perverse effects. It needs a different approach to operate effectively in the space of possibilities. I'm under no illusion that it's going to take a long time to change the way the organised vertical world works. We've got to find ways to mitigate, mediate and soften it. There are people who are doing this work, including your practice. My work is in what you call the community: how do we make these two worlds interact better?

OM   So what makes a community?

EC   It depends on the context. At the heart of community are the relationships between the people—how and why they've come together, what their motivations are. They can come together because they're suddenly in crisis or they have long-term interests of issues or identity, and are working together supportively. The key thing that makes it different from the institutional, organised world of work is that they have come together for very personal reasons and there's nobody obliging them to be together.

OM   There's now much more ability for peer-to-peer interactions to happen on a virtual scale. Has the dynamic or energy in those communities changed in respect of this shift?

EC   The organised vertical world can divide and rule because the horizontal peer world has poor information and so is often ineffective. My passion is to improve the quality and flow of information in the horizontal peer world and help develop organisational systems and methods to make that information more easily available, so the interventions from the horizontal peer world in the space of possibilities are more effective. New social media have created new opportunities. My interest is to use technology to complement face-to-face encounters. When it does this it can be much more effective. An example is in the uprising in Cairo: activists became visible through social media, but they had for many years been developing their human networks below the radar in shared conversations about their political and economic system. Social media did not cause the uprising, but the system of human relationships was made more effective when needed by the availability of the new social media.

OM   Do you have methods for measuring a success over a period of time?

EC   Not just with numbers. That is a vertical, mechanical approach. The qualitative data is shoehorned into something that serves another conceptual model. I'm not advocating that we can just drop our mechanical ways of thinking about organisation: it's the dominant mode and the default mode. But by definition you're predicting something which is unpredictable in a non linear living system. It needs a different approach using also intuition, the idea of emergence and a sensitivity to human relationships. I call myself a social gardener—I've got some ideas about how some things might evolve. I work to nurture the conditions within which they can.

OM Are there vital ingredients for what that condition or context is?

Patience, receptivity, listening, all the skills that are well understood in various areas of our society now, whether it's psychotherapy, good group management, facilitation. But they're not the dominant mode. Creating a viable space for people to operate is to be aware of what it is that makes people feel good about what they're offering freely, in their own spare time. If you don't do that, people will drift away quickly.

OM In terms of people coming together and something emerging in terms of a direction they may want to take, do you allow those things to develop as they do or do you intervene?

EC My method is to take it slowly. Things die when the wrong things are put together. Without much better working of the vertical hierarchical and horizontal peer systems, perhaps it will all get worse. In some places like Syria the vertical world is incapable of handling the messages, the pleas from this other system. They don't know how to do it. In the West our equivalent may be the global corporate world. Everyone, even the national government, is powerless to manage their own economies. They're different struggles, but we've got these two different kinds of human social systems now interacting with each other increasingly violently across the world. Unless we understand this and feed it into our analysis and into our growing methods of dealing with modern issues and problems, we're always going to trip up, whether we're in a dictatorship or a liberal democracy.

OM I believe the idea of progress is problematic: the battles are always the same but there's a different context, different methods and we're always having to work to have the smaller voices heard in the larger conversations.

EC I'm a great believer in the spiral view. They seem to go in circles but they're in a slightly different place the next time round. The human world is more complex than it was 100 years ago but often we face the same issues in a different context. There's quite a debate that goes on about gradual evolution or whether or not there's a bifurcation—whether there can be a big jump in physical evolution. Maybe the same debate can be had in terms of social organisation. Things are changing all the time and if we nurture the conditions as we can with the information we have and we may be able to shepherd things in the right direction, we can avoid some cataclysmic change. I have the pessimism of the intellect and optimism of the will on that.

OM What are the different motivations behind community engagement?

EC It depends. What is your definition of community engagement? Whose motivations? A linguistic illustration of this is when vertical hierarchal world talks about community engagement, their language is peppered with the word 'harness'. A straitjacket. If you start trying to harness the horizontal peer world you will absorb it and change it. So how do we enable this horizontal world to get its organisational act together so that when it meets the vertical hierarchical world and the space of possibilities, people from both systems can actually want to work together? The language should be: how do we tap into the horizontal peer world?

OM   **Do these two worlds need a third party or a conduit in order to communicate effectively?**

EC   Not necessarily, but when the vertical hierarchical world and the horizontal peer try to interact, they are helped with new insights, training systems and management understanding. Evolution happens in what scientists call the "adjacent possible"— by the next thing from where you're standing. It needs a change in attitude. No one of us has the solutions, and the problems are so immense. The organised technocratic vertical hierarchical world is now so powerful yet so enmeshed and under such deadlines that it can't change overnight. The most important thing, not the only thing, is understanding how it could be different and not expecting people to be able to implement change to achieve the desired result immediately.

OM   **Certain things can be accelerated if they're augmented with various media and technologies but you also need patience for relationships to develop and interact.**

EC   This is about community development. People have honed skills and understandings of all of this for the last 50 years, but we still haven't found a way for the vertical hierarchical world to use them effectively. Community development has been decimated in the last three years. The most successful community workers have been people with good people skills, who listen and help others to listen and understand each other to find their mutual interests, and have an understanding of the horizontal peer world. I offer my two systems model of the social ecosystems dance as an insight and tool to help achieve effective change through nurturing the conditions for emergence.

_____ **Mat Hunter**

Mat Hunter is Chief Design Officer at the Design Council where he
bridges the often too distant worlds of design and human interaction.
Hunter's current work is around demonstrating how design innovation
can affect social change and policy. This essay is the outcome of two
interviews with Hunter.

Creating a rich ecosystem for transformational design

There is always the opportunity to innovate. However,
innovation is dependent on whether there exists the
imperative for change and an accessible means of change.
In the case of policymakers, there is little capacity-building
for civil servants to interact with the public. This lack of
coherence and engagement with the people that they
affect challenges the relationship between the public and
their services. Changing this situation starts with empathy,
appropriating the social sciences around ethnography, to
try to understand what's going on in people's lives so as
to create policy responses that really work for them. Some
people argue that there is no received methodology on
policymaking, so part of the challenge is to include equipping
policymakers with tools in order to have a more structured
and human-centred way to create policy. These could include
visualisation and prototyping, for example. Currently, though,
the idea that design methods can shape structures and
solutions is still only embryonic.

One fall out from this is limited opportunities for experimental
design, or even conventional design. In the UK, a lot of
energy has been poured into evidence-based policies,
taking existing solutions to problems and analysing whether

they work in the ways that they were expected to. Proven
science takes precedent over untested theory or practice,
such as in the case of randomised control trials, and for
as long as policymakers lack the confidence to risk an
alternative approach to developing solutions, design won't
be implemented at this stage. What we argue at the Design
Council is that both approaches are complementary. In
the early days you can't run randomised controlled trials
for everything. You have to use an iterative approach of
working with people, until you want to scale a project or
idea up, and then it becomes imperative to use various
forms of objective evaluation.

In this respect codesign is important because of the
complexity of what needs to be designed and the diverse
skills and perspectives required. In addition, places and
services (unlike products) require ongoing collaboration to
be successful—where would Virgin Atlantic be without its
staff that believed in the brand? Where would a community
centre be without the community who wanted to inhabit
it? Therefore codesign is both about creating the right
end product but also about bringing along a community
of interest so they feel ownership of the process. In local

government more people understand design than ever before; they understand that they have a community that is finite and very tangible outside their front door and they have to find new ways to engage with them. This is, however, harder to do in central government.

In most scenarios the best solution is to embed a talented designer in a team of other professionals to bring out the best in people and to take responsibility for the overall experience. There is still such a thing as talent and still such a thing as practice—a talented, practised individual will always be more capable than the opposite. But, at the same time, designers do not have total ownership over creativity.

Front line professionals have the capacity and training to be good innovators, but they are wedded to the day-to-day and find it hard to have headspace to innovate. Inserting a designer into that space, who has got a slightly different skillset, is useful in helping to catalyse change in this group of professionals.

The ultimate successes are totally provable and therefore quantitative. It is evidence-based and very much about the impact on people's lives. It takes time and money, yet even before this stage there may be indicators of success. One of the devices that we incubated is called Ode, which stimulates appetite in people with dementia. When a sufferer forgets to eat, it can lead to crisis: expensive managed care or hospitalisation. The thesis is that to have the best quality of life and reduce the cost to family and state, you should stay at home as long as possible and be as resilient as you can. If malnutrition is a particular problem, then this device creates high-quality food fragrances to stimulate the appetite. It allows the user an opportunity to be resilient.

The classic paradigm of design thinking, as explored by the designers of Ode and design author and thinker Roger Martin, is that rather than having just two choices—the expensive human option and the cheap inhuman option—we should think about how we can create a cost-effective hybrid human-technology option that both feels good and is highly productive. So part of the challenge is, as always, about designing great things.

In my experience, designers view systemic change as a piece-by-piece building process that requires architectural acts to create the platforms. It doesn't happen overnight. There is proof all around us that there is a need for top-down approaches, but also bottom-up collaboration. Without both

working simultaneously you would not be able to have an exceptionally rich ecosystem of professionals and users to effect transformative design.

In theory self-service should be a complete insult, but sometimes we actually like it when it can give us a little more control. So how can I have more control over my healthcare, for example? This is a big theme. It is not for everyone—there are people who are lonely and worried, so we have to think about how they will want to come in and talk through things. But for many others there may be digital means to get to my GP that take less time. You have to overcome it—to do that is to make stuff quickly. You do it by demonstration rather than by persuasion.

So codesign can often speak to the emotional state of the participants. The interesting thing about services is that they require human interaction to make them successful and therefore, if that's the case, the general expense of positive emotional attitude of people will be important.

The anecdotal space at the beginning—the earliest benefit of that codesign approach—is about getting people predisposed to and emotionally positive towards something. The more we then progress, the more those emotions and subjective attitudes will be seen as imparting the right answer. Irrespective of codesign, the question is: does the intervention work? Are people just wasting their time? Is this a really good solution?

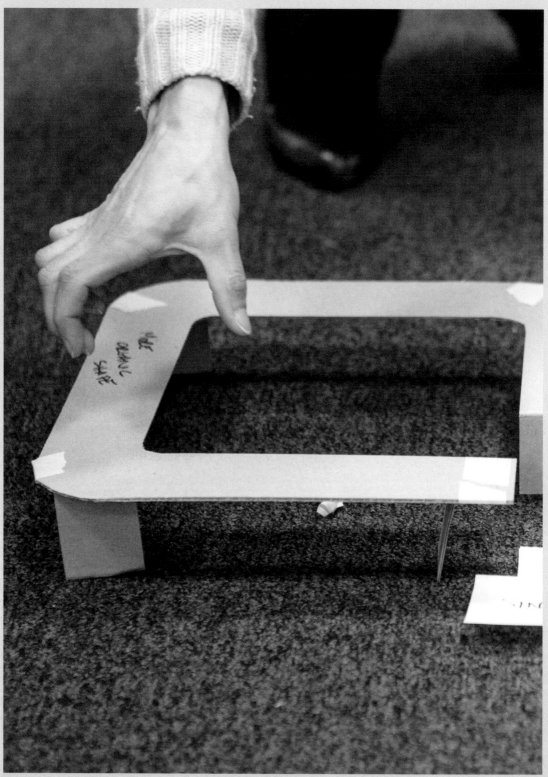

_____ Jeremy Myerson

Jeremy Myerson began his career as a design journalist in the 1980s, drawn to the proliferation of workspaces throughout London. He soon identified a lack of interest in and discussion around user-centred design, so in 1986 he launched the influential magazine, Design Week. Myerson is currently Director and Helen Hamlyn Chair of Design, at the Helen Hamlyn Centre for Design, a user-centred research centre at the RCA in London, which he cofounded in 1999. This is an excerpt from an interview with TILT.

Design is a process, not a product

OM   **We believe that everyone is creative, and can engage meaningfully in a design process. Do you agree? Does this mean the nature and need for design is changing?**

JM   I don't believe that everybody is creative. I believe the nature of creativity is the ability to have novel or innovative ideas. Everyone has the ability to articulate ideas and the right to engage in a design process. If designers accept that, then the nature of design changes. I think it's a subtle change from designing for people to designing with people.

OM   **Is the term 'innovation' now synonymous with design? How do you understand what is meant by the term 'innovation'?**

JM   I have a very simple approach to this. Creativity is the generation of new ideas. Innovation is the implementation of new ideas. Innovation is taking new ideas and realising them, in the marketplace or built form. Design is the bridge between creativity and innovation. Design is how you go from creativity to innovation. Design is a process not a product.

OM   **How do you see the focus of so-called 'innovation' as part of the designer's skillset? Is it something only designers can do?**

JM   No. I think scientists, writers and architects innovate. Anyone can be innovative in any field. Innovation is part of the designer's skillset. It is the result of designers taking ideas and giving them form and organisation and meaning, and articulating and visualising them and making them real.

OM   **We're convinced that transdisciplinarity is a key component of successful design teams. How do you put together the team at the Helen Hamlyn Centre?**

JM   We tend to have social scientists in our teams, as well as engineers. They're very collaborative and design with people as opposed to for people. In the middle of hard and soft science you have designers who are skilled at prototyping, visualising and creating probes so they can talk to people.

OM   **How did you come to this—did you identify the types of disciplines you needed or was it more organic than that?**

JM   It's been organic—trial and error—and evolved over many years. We were less interdisciplinary a few years ago. The growth area is to do with anthropology, ethnography and psychology. It's the soft sciences that have grown in our space. That's the pendulum swing. Most of the metaphors in management are engineering-oriented. What's happened is that trend is away from management-led design towards people-centred design and that's why the social sciences have risen.

OM   **Are people making room for this within businesses and existing systems?**

JM   I think so. If you look in design consultancies, there are more people with social science backgrounds and I think architects and designers were interested in urban planning metaphors and now they're increasingly interested in social science patterning, in ethnographic research and in how people behave. A lot of the most interesting writers on office design are from this background, like Jacqueline Vischer, a French-Canadian psychologist. A book by Susan Cane called *Quiet* (2012), which is an attack on the extrovert ideal, rather the nature of the introvert, is really interesting. There's a section on why modern offices are so bad because they promote the extrovert ideal in an open-plan space: everyone's gabbing and no one can get work done.

OM   **Systemic change is needed, whether that be around sustainability, people-centred approaches, or simply making things better. How do you think systemic change comes about? From small interventions, or from top-down macro shifts?**

JM   It all depends on who bears the costs of sustainable initiatives—is it the company or the staff?—and making some sacrifices where both shoulder the burden. It's a campaigning culture. At the opposite end, where nobody is doing much, it's a pragmatic culture. Systemic change is interesting because I think office design is getting more like the fashion business—there's a couture high end that everyone looks at and the big companies show stuff at NeoCon. Most office design is at the high street, but there's this couture stuff that's influential and perculates down gradually. The big problem about office design is the way buildings are put up, a very low common denominator spec, for example with grids and lights. Offices are badly overlit. I don't think we'll get systemic change until we change how offices are built, financed and let. It is changing. There's some interesting property companies around. The systemic change that's required for a people-centred approach is not something that designers can achieve themselves—it's got to happen at a much higher level of capital investment in property.

OM **So the agents of change will always be top-down?**

JM Organisations, and business and property investment. You can influence that process but you can never wrest control from it. There is a very lively fringe in the coworking movement that is having an effect. You can see some great plays at the Edinburgh Festival but it's not going to change the commercial rubbish in the West End. Change is happening all the time, it's a patchwork. But for the mainstream to change you've got to affect how buildings are made: why create office space? What are the investment decisions? The big thing is repurposing, it's really important. There's a surplus of space, it's expensive to build. People are realising it's better refurbishing something existing in the middle of London or Manhattan than stick everyone out on a business park in Queens.

OM **Is there an opportunity to question how public policy decisions are made, supplanting statistical validation with something more nuanced, emergent and complex? Does design play a role in this challenge?**

JM Public policy decision-making is already nuanced, emergent and complex. Design has a role to play in explaining and exploring public policy decision-making by prototyping new ideas. I'm less confident around workplace design than I am around healthcare or education because there doesn't seem to be a government policy on it. It's the Wild West of rampant free-market capitalism. Workplaces have to have more value than just a place to rest your papers. You've got to deal with issues like territory, belonging, identity, self-worth. A lot of offices are good at functional comfort, where they go next is psychological comfort, which is why codesigning is so important.

TILT was founded in 2010 by Oliver Marlow and Dermot Egan. Having previously worked independently, Marlow as a filmmaker and designer and Egan as a social entrepreneur, they later collaborated on implementing coworking environments for The Hub. Deciding to put their codesign strategies into practice, Marlow and Egan established TILT as an innovative architecture and design studio.

What makes a space enabling?

Space is a conversation. It is not merely a container for people and things. Instead, space is ever evolving and iterative. With this in mind, TILT has developed a dialectic between the space and the end-user. It is a conversation with the people who will ultimately demand the space to perform in specific ways, who will be affected by that space and who will in turn affect it. This is the basis of codesign; a method for design rooted in an age-old appreciation of the value of inclusion.

Inclusivity. Participation. User-centred design. As these terms have come to mean an appendage to a consultative process that rarely reflects external voices, community concerns and future inhabitants' aspirations, there has been a backlash against them as design approaches, and instead they imply empty rhetoric. While this is not an entirely unreasonable conclusion to draw, these are the approaches that, if handled correctly, have the capacity to shift the perception of design from being elitist, alienating and something that happens to people, to being accessible, emotive and something that people can feel ownership towards. One important aspect of codesign is to combat wilful ignorance by bringing all the stakeholders of a project into the process from the start.

Codesign is characterised by a multiplicity of voices. It makes room for identities to form through action and reflection. The dialectic is part of a convergent and divergent pattern, almost as a breathing rhythm, and exists in opposition to conventional societal values that tend to commodify experience and limit relativity. Rather, the codesign approach opens up dialogue between disparate stakeholders in any given organisation or system. Using workshops in which specific activities are introduced, TILT's aim is to engage the end-user's sensory and cognitive perceptions. Rooted in the practice of performance and environmental artists from the 1960s and 1970s, this approach stimulates innate creativity among groups of people, many of whom would otherwise not believe they possessed such talent, or at least had little experience in accessing or sharing it. Codesign explodes preconceptions held about current design process, as the participant's involvement is highly valued and re-presented in increasingly formalised, evaluated material throughout. Their experiences are aggregated into graphic representations in an ongoing dialectic that results in a design brief and ultimately into a finished space.

This process relies on a level of fluidity inherent in group dynamics yet the workshops structure this informal gathering to build something appropriate, distinct, purposeful, loved and sustainable that is also meaningful to its users. While it has become the norm for designers and architects to prescribe spaces to functions and instruct people in what they need for their business, civic buildings, public squares or homes, TILT has pared back the design process and begins by listening to the client and the user. This allows TILT—and the participants—to identify the individuals who have a vested interest in the outcome. From here, a cultural and community context can surface. The design brief doesn't come directly from this, but is drawn from the synthesis of participants' ideas and responses—emotional and practical— that arise during the orchestrated activities.

Moving between community and individual, TILT's creative process is marked by intensive conversations and excursions that invite the everyday to filter into the sometimes abstract and playful workshop activities. The motivation for all contributors on any project is that they are being listened to and that within this forum there are substantive results that they can own. Enabling a better comprehension and clarity of intent compared to design-in-isolation, codesign sets the tone for a wider, discursive process to unfold. Indeed, if the role of the designer is not as the sole author of a space, but is partly a conduit for systemic variants, a facilitator of implicit creativity and an amplifier for multiple voices, it is within this framework that the client and participants can directly affect the final outcome.

Though it may be obvious to state that environments can be transformative and empowering, as has been demonstrated in the recent protests in public squares across New York, Cairo and Istanbul, equally, the same spaces can be oppressive and intimidating, and used to control and abuse power. Too often civic architecture and urban planning must contend with economic-political agendas beyond serving the public; they are therefore rarely genuinely public and owners have done little to incorporate social and cultural diversity. Indeed, the current system is not working in the best interests of the people it is meant to serve. What TILT is concerned with is improving how these spaces, buildings, furniture and services are designed to better serve their function and reinstate public space to be shaped by the people who use it. Borrowing from Jürgen Habermas' notion of deliberative democracy, this approach creates a forum for discussion that will reflect the most appropriate end, as it fosters an egalitarian community of autonomous agents.

Part of this resistance to codesign as a serious design approach stems from the architecture profession's master-builder tradition that supports a level of elitism and from which unnecessary obstacles are put in the way of meaningful public participation. For TILT this forward-looking scenario poses no threat to designers and architects, only distinguishes their role as an evolving one. While architecture standards demand a level of commitment to public consultation, there is little regulation that ties an architect or designer to incorporating the contributions put forward by the future inhabitants or owners. In seeking to establish a discursive practice of transdisciplinary professionals, TILT has been freed from many constraints or expectations set by the industry, and has therefore been able to explode the conventional design process through its codesign method. From this privileged position, it has become clear that between the formal system—decision-makers—and the informal system—communities and individuals, or end-users—there is an interstice, a 'differend' (so-called by Jean-François Lyotard) where there is room to effect social change. So the codesign approach that TILT employs for each project sits within this interstitial space, and seeks to re-evaluate the chronic lack of cohesion and dialogue between the top-down and grassroots approaches.

Providing a platform to involve the users in the design process involves various risks. What if the numerous voices turn into white noise and the crowd becomes confusing, lacking cohesion? How do you create a scenario in which the primary motive of inclusion and collusion informs a structure that then gives way to a tangible outcome? How does a room full of people become a community? How can we enable people who feel intimidated by the design process to be an agent in demystifying it? How do you foster ownership?

Far from conclusive, TILT's ambition is not to answer these questions but to ask them throughout every project. They are the foundations for an investigation that brings diversity into the fold, rather than attempting to homogenise it. Pertinent to the codesign approach is an understanding that it is the people that use the space who give purpose to it, who activate and animate it with their encounters and insights, and who imbue it with meaning. With this in mind, it has become imperative to develop a way to engage those people, the end-users in a process that embeds their ideas, ambitions and creativity into the final product, be it a building, a space, furniture or services. It is these people who know best what they need from design. This endows the designer with a role unlike the one that is traditionally expected; it requires the designer to work with intuition and to facilitate creativity and cultivate existing tensions into productive contributions. Inside the metaphorical suitcase is a considered and ever-growing array of practical action-based stimuli, each appropriate for different design stages but not all applicable at any one time. The balance of their use and combination relies on intuition as much as experience.

In an ongoing effort to ensure that this is the core of TILT's practice, rather than a notional consultation or tick-box addendum, TILT has evolved a method to foster a genuine participatory design process through codesign. The approach invites curiosity and adapts to new scenarios to foster a fluid and dynamic process. Set within an overarching framework of Listening, Creating and Making, TILT employs this suitcase of dialectical activities to stimulate engagement at different scales and with different ambitions. TILT's role is in inscribing the experiences and conversations of the participants onto a spatial context. The following pages show some of the activities from the many TILT has developed. They are presented alongside projects and experiences that help ground the work, showing both processes and also finished spaces. They afford some context to this practice-based methodology and help to visually map the rhythmical dialectic implicit in codesign.

Practice

Activity Location _____

Mapping relationships is a key element of codesign. Spaces can be usefully defined as zones of activity, some crossing over, others more distinct. By bringing together the interrelationships of space and use one can get a dynamic picture of an organisation. By then plotting the multiple locations of these activities, a three-dimensional picture emerges that adds depth to this dynamic picture and offers myriad insights into an organisation's identity and aspirations.

Independent thoughts
Using Activity Location with the team from creative agency Independents United really helped us plan their London office and maximise flexibility through the use of mobile furniture elements. They really understood the value of documenting the design process and employed a member of their team to video the codesign workshops.

The value of outputs

Creating outputs from the codesign activities that can be presented back to clients is a key part of the codesign process. It reinforces the message that the input is valued and helps to develop the narrative of the space. From this output the Independents United team learned the importance of the kitchen space as a location of activity, which subsequently led them to include it in the design.

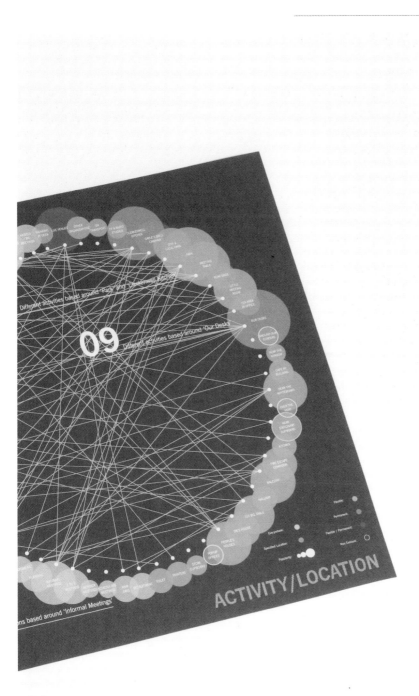

Troika

The office we designed for Troika encapsulates how possible it is to accommodate a number of design elements simultaneously within a relatively small space. Formal meeting, informal meeting, kitchen, touchdown working, fixed working and storage elements are all addressed here in a 100 square metre space. The extract from our workshop outputs shows the developing relationships activated through this process.

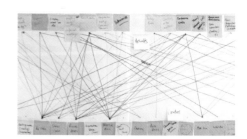

Mobile meeting

The desire to have small private meetings and/or calls without permanently dividing the office emerged during our codesign workshops with the Independents United team. This led directly to the design of the Cariola, a fully powered and ventilated mobile meeting pod. It's not uncommon to gain inspiration for product ideas from codesign workshops.

Ask the Space _____

The intuitive and emotional responses one has to the atmosphere
of a space often go unrecorded, but they are essential to consider
when designing space. Participants are asked to think about
the landscape of spatial contrasts and comparisons while they
converse with the space. What is conversing with the space?
We're opening up a dialogue between you and the space,
creating an opportunity for conversation.

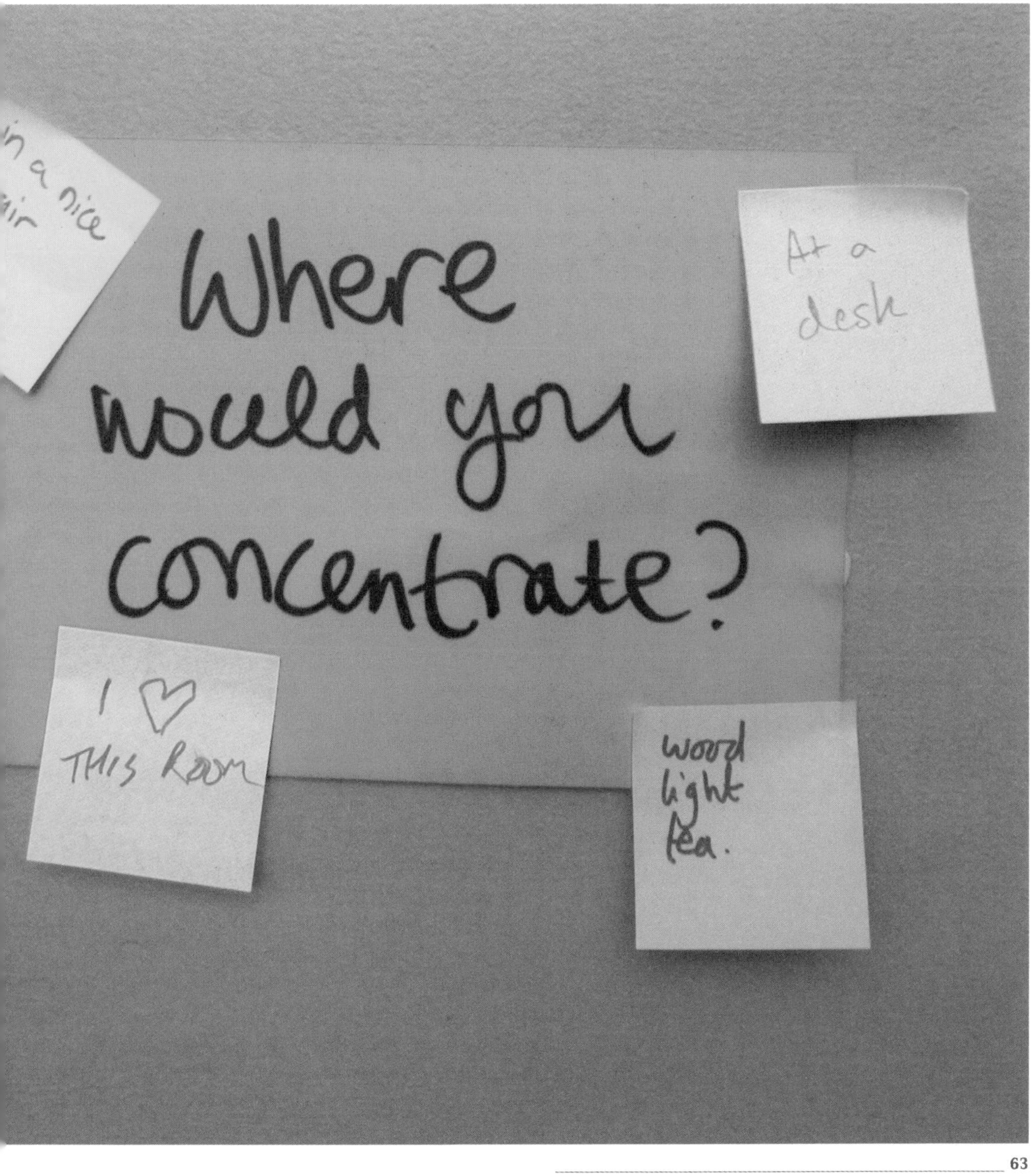
in a nice
Where would you concentrate?
At a desk
I ♡ THIS ROOM
wood
light
tea.

Crowdsourcing at the Southbank

From the bricks for the seating to the bottles for the lights, this snug space and bar area were designed for the Southbank Centre's Festival Village using almost entirely recycled materials sourced by the participant community themselves. It's a good demonstration of how opening up the design process can unlock the latent energy of a community.

Codesign is multilingual

Above we can see a man writing a response to the question "Where does the kitchen go?" written in Italian. Codesign reaches across cultures as it taps into our innate curiosity and desire to participate.

Codesign in the Amazon

This is Natura's new knowledge and innovation centre in Manaus, deep in the Brazilian Amazon. The codesign process brought together scientists and researchers from the company with local medical practitioners to foster knowledge exchange. It was a great success and, while the space doesn't look much different to a traditional office, an embedded culture of collaboration is at its heart.

Library Chairs

As with all TILT products, the ideas for developing the Library Chair were inspired by needs expressed during the codesign that weren't being answered by the furniture market. In this instance the community wanted a library in a Grade II listed building where they couldn't hang shelves. Our response was to put the library into the chairs, creating Library Chairs.

Blind Lead

Creating insights around space use through live prototyping helps us to better understand how to design the space. In Blind Lead a team directs a participant through a scenario in the space. Not only are we looking at spatial narrative but we are thinking about how our visual sense informs so much of our experience of space.

Lead on
Blind Lead works equally well in any language and amongst different age groups. Here we have members of a coworking space in Syracuse, Italy, participating in the activity. In the background you can see the criss-crossing of string from previous participants who have left their mark in the space.

Sound waves
Activities inform many design outcomes. At the Festival Village, the lounge of the space, known as the Hearth, had sound absorption suspended from the ceiling after participants explored sound with the space through the Blind Lead activity. The floor was also raised to give the Hearth a different acoustic to the rest of the space.

Surface history

Blind Lead provides a completely different sensory experience of space. It disorientates participants and gives them an alternative perspective. It works particularly well in spaces with variable heights and interesting material surfaces. When we used it for the codesign of the listed Student Hub building in Oxford, the activity helped engage participants with the history of the building in a unique way.

String theory

Different colour strings reflect participants' pathways through the space. The interwoven trailing strings create an interesting fleeting narrative. In this version of the Blind Lead activity we conducted in the Student Hub building, the coloured strings were laid out with a separate instruction, giving each group a different journey to navigate within the building.

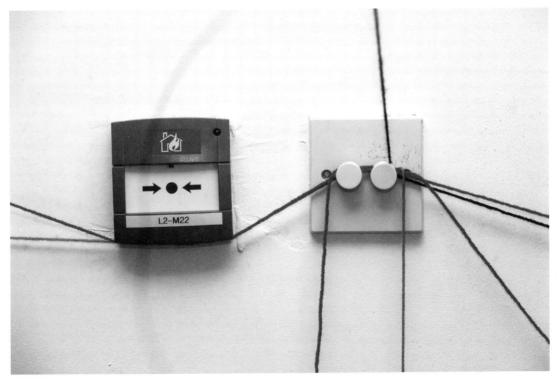

Desk Top _____

A desktop says so much about a person: how they work, what they need, where they place things. Working with a team, or multiple teams, it's possible to draw comparisons and conclusions about an organisation's workflow and prioritise. It may not even be a desk—work is more mobile, more flexible now, but we still need a place to work, we still need a 'desktop'.

Coworking

This coworking space we designed in Chiswick, London, provides for numerous work 'states', including touchdown informal working, longer-stay concentrated working and dedicated private working. Members choose the desk and location that best suits their working style, which may change throughout the day or week. This shift towards providing activity areas is directly influencing the growth of Activity Based Working.

Suitcase Desk

For a number of people a personalised workstation is important. This group are drawn to the dynamic nature and community vibe of coworking spaces but still want to retain a sense of privacy. This need inspired the Suitcase Desk, a contemporary take on the classic bureau design, allowing users a secure lockable, self-contained, private work space. When locked, it offers a flat surface that any coworker can use, maximising space.

Dodecahedron _____

One of the most interesting approaches to design principles in recent years has come from the permaculture movement. Working from patterns and the juxtaposition of contrasting and compatible elements, it is a fascinating way to design.

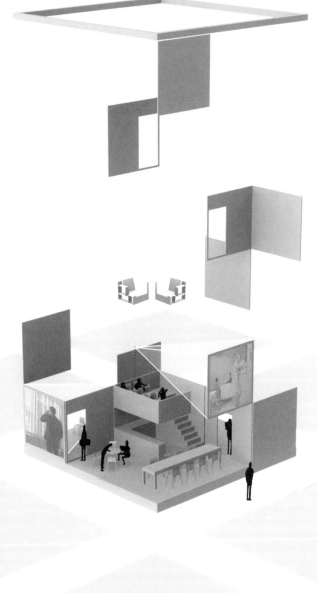

The Hanging Room

The Hanging Room is a spatial experiment into the workplace of the future. We are fascinated by programmable spaces, the improvised and flexible. Utilising projection, mobile screens and furniture, we deployed the concept at the 100% Design show as part of the 2013 London Design Festival.

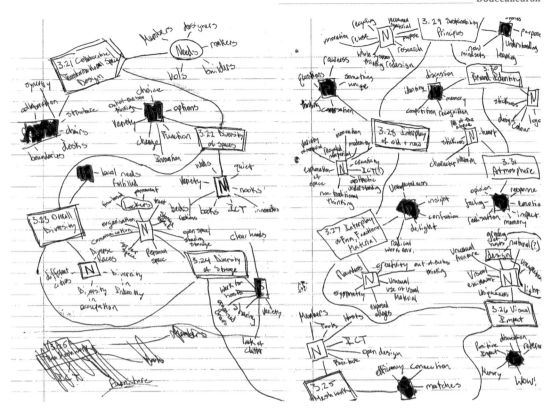

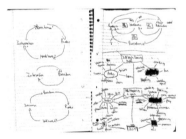

Always working

Like any project, creating and iterating the codesign tools requires time and energy. We will often start, like here, scribbling thoughts across pages before we can hone, test and clarify a clear structure and flow. We always do this in real environments, and as part of our projects. We are lucky to work with clients who love to be a part of this innovative R&D model.

Ecology Map

Finding ways to sort, shape and prioritise information and insights as part of a design day is an integral exercise. Understanding relationships visually, whether between metaphorical or literal things, is an important step to thinking spatially. It helps to create the stories of the community and highlights the complementary and overlapping functions that inform the design of the space.

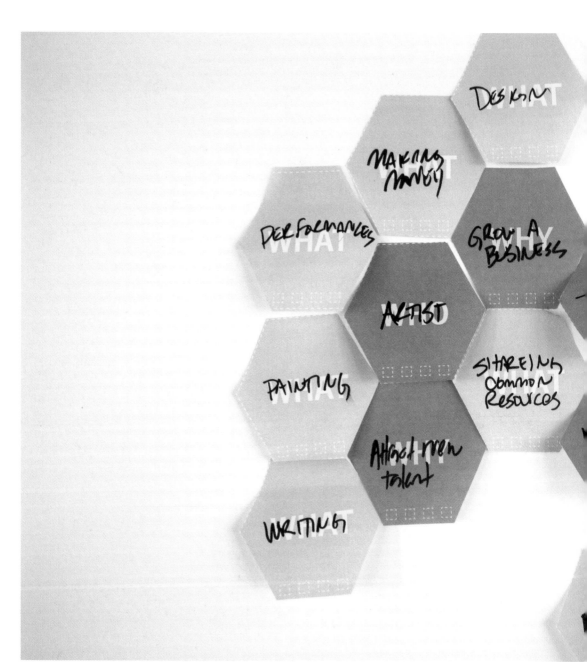

Space as a story
Ecology Maps create a story of the space. The 'who' is our character, the 'what' our action and the 'why' our motivation. A complex spatial topography requires an associative approach like this. These three images are from a coworking space in Las Vegas, The Festival Village in London, and the Oxford Hub. They are all complex buildings and all needing a narrative methodology with many layers and associations.

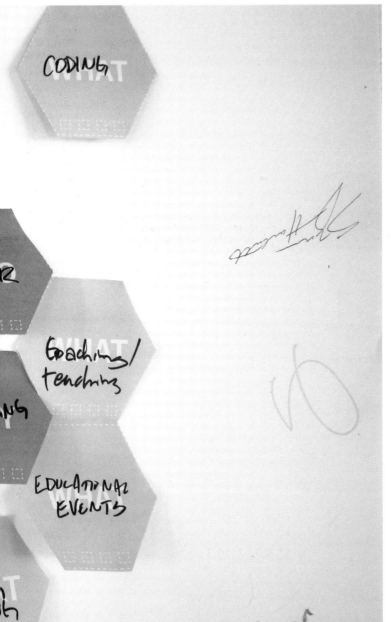

Come together

Linking emergent themes together and giving them a priority is key to creating a sense of purpose for a space. Part of the challenge of the activity is to find ways to visually sort information. The approach in the picture above is to use three corners, each themed, and then find the patterns. This picture is taken at an early stage; time is needed to sort and re-sort and find the best associations.

Flexible systems
This Instagram shows 300 members of the
Simón Bolívar Orchestra enjoying food at
the Festival Village. The fact that this space
could cater for them while simultaneously
accommodating so many other functions is a
testament to how it was collectively conceived
and delivered. The map of Festival Village
shows the intention behind the space, allowing
it to cater for different usage states. The
orchestra are occupying the two yellow strips.

White space ▪
Cafe ▪
Canteen ▪
Kitchen/bar ▪
Cinema ▪
Live music ▪
Exhibition ▨
Hearth ▪
Meeting and coworking ▨

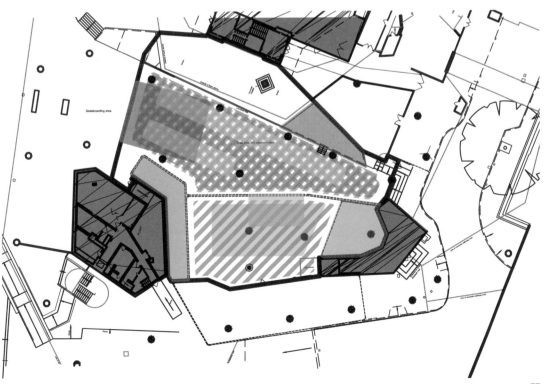

Placemaking _____

Codesigning with communities can begin well before a space or location has been identified. Particularly with coworking, it is most successful when it is community first, space second. How to choose that space and decide what elements are essential is a crucial part of this. We use Placemaking in order to help teams identify these elements in a detailed manner, creating a framework to integrate vision with inevitable compromise.

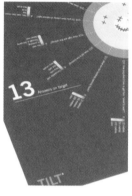

Answers on target
When considering a potential location, it should be cross-referenced against the important questions that the community regard as fundamental to its success. In the output for this activity a map is created highlighting the spectrum of responses to particular questions.

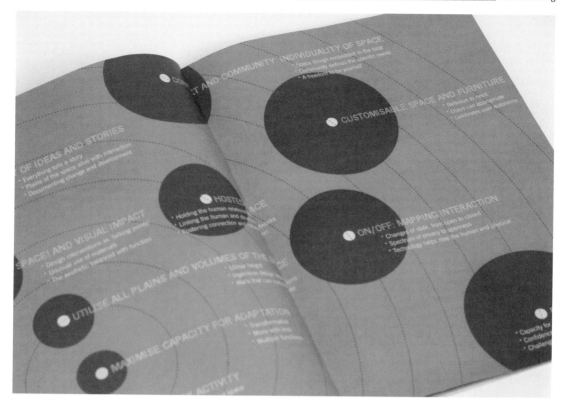

Space principles

For our project with Devon Work Hubs, a rural network of coworking spaces established by Devon County Council, we worked with space owners in the region to explore the ideal coworking space to suit the local context. The output was combined with other elements to develop a design handbook.

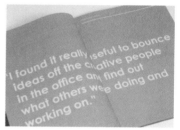

"I found it really useful to bounce ideas off the creative people in the office and find out what others were doing and working on."

Flags

Enacting spatial distinction by using props provides a community with a means to manifest their thoughts quickly and intuitively. The props can be anything—the size of a table worked up in chalk, the location of services written on card, or the positions of windows marked by two people standing close by. Working outside, ideally on the site of the new building, or in a space large enough to hold this prototyping, is a great way to bring the space to life, walk through, roleplay and mock up in quick time.

Design speaks

The finished space has the capacity to offer visual references that reinforce the spatial distinctions defined during the initial codesign workshops. At the Student Hub space in Oxford, we used colours on the doors to denote different functions within the rooms and to provide intuitive wayfinding.

Human markers

During a project to design a youth hub with London-based charity Global Generation, we asked workshop participants to hold signs with different spatial elements on them and moved them around as required to explore layouts. Using participants as markers in this way can work really well both as a way to engage them in the activity but also to give them a very real sense of the space.

Following ─────────────────────

Service design is a crucial element of what we do, but we flip the process on its head. We use the space as the tool, creating narratives and ecologies so the spatial design meshes perfectly with the services and experiences of the space. It is a powerful combination, and an activity like Following, much more than a simple user journey or user touchpoint, helps create those narratives.

I can see you

During our codesign of the Whittington Hospital Pharmacy in London, we shadowed patients and staff to share their experience through the prescription dispensing process. One thing we noticed was that patients got bored and frustrated waiting for prescriptions. This led us to expose the workings of the pharmacy robot so they could observe their orders being fulfilled.

Freeze Frame _____

The flow of our workshops incorporates as many forms of
learning and expression as we can manage. We need always
to tailor the codesign to the users, and each user is different.
By moving seamlessly from words and discussion to images
and drawing creates the opportunity to activate various
perspectives in a group, and therefore get the most from
their input.

Making it real
Sometimes you have to encourage participants
to really imagine how a space will be used
and translate those scenarios visually. When
the scenarios are presented together a picture
of the space emerges. Using Freeze Frame
with young people is particularly effective.

Workspace or lecture seating?

Mocking up a point in time for a space helps to formalise multifunctionality. Hubs often have a bandstand conceived as touchdown meeting space, and seating for events. These principles of adaptability, responsiveness and flexibility are crucial. We supported the design of Hub Vienna, working with Michael Stor and Alex Riegler, while in Zurich supporting Antonio Scarponi.

Give Get _____

Exploring collective intelligence and insight is one thing, but exploring the networks of expertise, resources and abilities within a community can create very powerful ways to deliver low budget community-based projects. Simultaneously it meshes community and creates means for skill sharing, fostering legacy and resilience. We would ask, "what would you give?" and "what would you like to get?" This reciprocity is at the root of comaking, and at the heart of resilient communities.

Get what you give
Give Get ensures that we are utilising the talents of the community and offering people the opportunity to contribute and participate where they would most like. Working with Global Generation, volunteers from across a number of organisations, including the Guardian Media Group, donated their time to join forces with the young people to help comake the space. Other companies, such as Interface, donated materials. The picture at the bottom of the adjacent page shows furniture sourced for the Oxford Hub through similar tactics.

Special treatment

The commitment that participants give to the codesign process, often without financial reward, can be humbling to see, and nowhere was this better illustrated than at the Festival Village at the Southbank Centre. We are always trying to develop ways to acknowledge a community, and here an exhibition was presented in the space while the exterior welcome sign collated hundreds of Instagrams of the project itself. It was an idea brought to life by Lyn Atelier, TILT's design partner on the project.

Image Blast _____

An activity in three parts, collage, virtual or self-directed.
For the latter, participants will have previously spent time
taking pictures on smartphones, cataloguing things they've
seen or elements that could work in their space. They can
then sort, creating thematic moodboards, detailing location
of activities, zonal interplay and look and feel.

My space/our space

For the Image Blast activity with the Student
Hub space, the participants used printouts of
images that they had collected and uploaded
to a shared Dropbox folder over the previous
weeks. They were encouraged to synthesise
the images into a collective output, blending
the personal into the social, and helping to
create a communal visual brief for the space.

Collective moodboard

The output of Image Blast produces a collective
moodboard, a useful visual reference for the
design as it progresses.

Storyboards

This collection of photos is from a workshop with Global Generation, with which we codesigned and comade a pop-up youth centre on the Argent site in Kings Cross, London. In contrast to the Image Blast at Student Hub, this group used images from magazines to create collages that spoke of the themes that they wanted reflected in their space.

Bottles and whisks

One of the great things about engaging people in codesign is harvesting the great ideas that emerge. The idea to use whisks as lampshades for the Festival Village proved inspired as they were easy and cheap to make and dispersed light very effectively. Likewise, the use of recycled glass Perrier bottles worked well, giving a colourful and elegant effect.

Bringing images to life

Collating images can have a very practical
function on a project. With the Festival Village at
the Southbank Centre, the images collected fed
directly into the development of the brief for the
lighting, and ultimately to the design of the lights
themselves. These lights went on to be produced
by the participants during the comaking.

Imaginary Tables _____

Deciding on a place to work is an opportunity to begin the discussion about how space is perceived. Why not incorporate the simple mechanics of codesign into the wider practice of spatial transformation? Creating imaginary tables gives the participants both a blank canvas and a framework within which to create.

What makes a table?
Even at the very beginning of the codesign process, Imaginary Tables is often one of the first activities we do. We are building towards opportunities where participants can get involved in the materiality of their environments, even making the tables themselves when required. The process takes time but there is nothing like direct engagement with the actual objects one will then live around.

Ground control

Sometimes the concept of an activity and how it is executed can directly inspire our design. The idea of using the floor as a tool to infer meaning led directly to the creation of a colour-coded visual map on the floor of the Festival Village to denote different space configurations. This helped to guide the users on how the space, and the furniture within it, needed to be arranged to maximise function and flexibility.

Making do
Another way to create a workshop setting is to appropriate what is around. Each specific table here, including the one yet to be made, is intended to shift perception of one's environment. As part of this particular workshop the types of table were included as a subject for later discussion around function and aesthetics.

In Place _____

A space that fulfils civic needs has to tick many boxes; we need to map access by various transports, the distance to the downtown core, proximity to amenities, access to clients and colleagues, proximity to/availability of green space, availability of parking, safety and security. Lastly, and most importantly, where do we live in respect of the space?

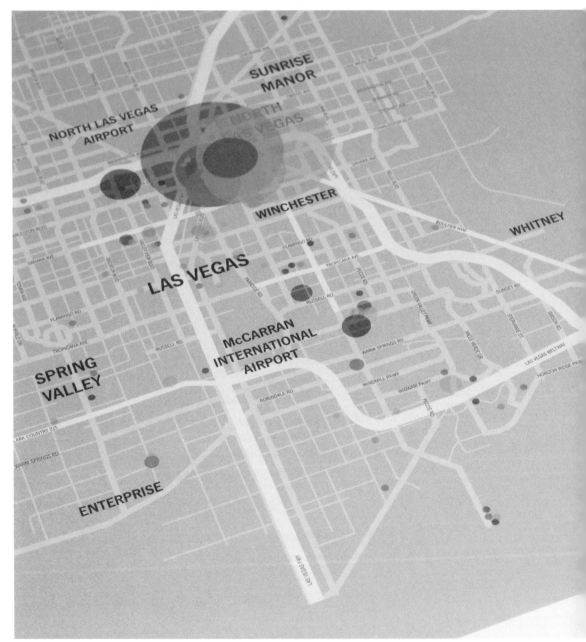

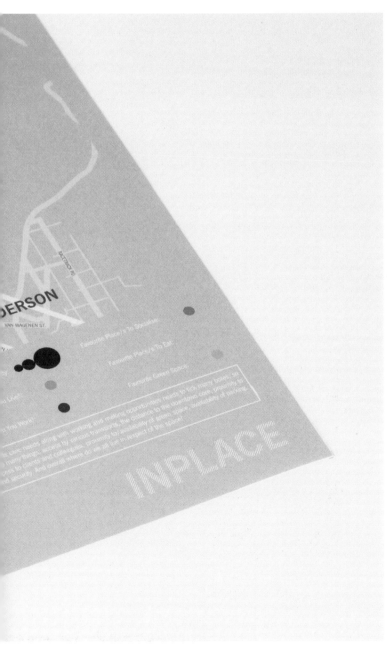

Knowing your place

The In Place activity encourages a community to map themselves and their favourite places through their personal geography. It's an activity that we've used repeatedly, including with the Downtown Project in Las Vegas. The output associated with In Place uses coloured spots in the graphic to represent various densities and situate the site we are working on in a wider context.

Landscapes _____

Designing space as a mesh of complementary and contrasting landscapes helps one to imagine the needs of the community in that space, and the relationship of activities. One is looking for a cohesive blend, as one would find in nature, hence the use of cartographic terms. We have to pay close attention to the thresholds between the landscapes, since these contact points both hold the space together and, if ill-conceived, pull it apart.

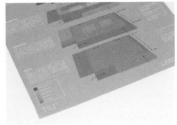

Shifting landscapes
As with a natural landscape, space can transition over time. At the coworking space we designed for Club Workspace in London's Bankside, the requirements of the space demanded that it change its function from touchdown coworking to events space as necessary. This influenced not only the design of the space but also the choice of furniture and signage within it.

Line Up

Knowing who's there, along with a light exploration into their networks, helps the design process keep focused on a real-life group of users. Asking people to photograph each other as they get set up for the day helps break the ice. The images themselves are then an integral part of the outputs of the codesign, giving identity and shape to the many insights and ideas that come up.

Photo exhibition
The pictures taken serve as nametags but can also be exhibited at and after the workshop to give a sense of the community involved. During the workshop at the Hub Kings Cross, staff and members had fun with the activity and learned new things about each other through the process.

Workers party

The Line Up activity isn't confined to workshops conducted during the Listening and Creating stages of the codesign. It can also be used during comake days in the Making phase. Group shots can complement images of individuals to build up the community profile. These are shots taken on site during the comake days on the Global Generation project, where we engaged volunteers to build the Youth Hub. Experienced builders worked side by side with volunteers and novices.

People power

Our graphical outputs are simple and elegant yet dense with information. The size of the images, the colours, quantities and connections all reveal insight about a community.

Make My Day _____

Understanding how a space will be used over time informs the needs of the design. To be able to explore and catalogue the activities, contexts and interactions that a user of a space will experience over the course of a day helps us to be definitive about the needs of that space. By expanding that time period to include the rhythms of a week, a month, or over seasons—even over the lifetime of a building—adds further insight.

Shaping the programme

Inviting workshop participants to piece together a potential day in the life of the space really helps to decipher how the space itself needs to transition. It also challenges the group to reflect on what is reasonably possible and what compromises may need to be made. Many of the ideas that emerged directly informed the programming for the space. At the Student Hub workshop useful events suggestions such as a social enterprise event fair and a series of documentary screenings were put forward and the community subsequently worked to implement them.

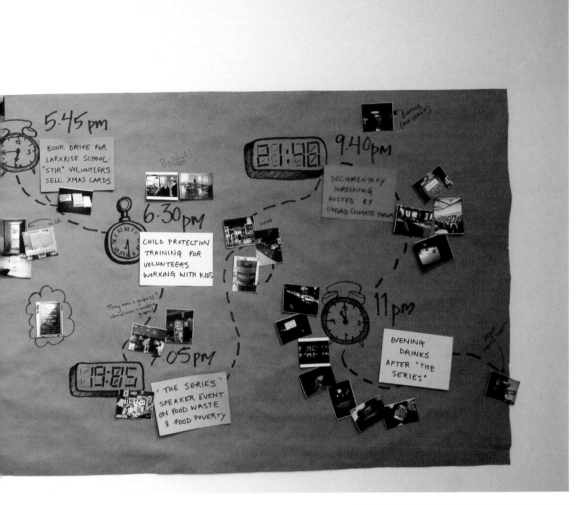

Mixing time

Once you start to properly understand the use of space throughout the day from different perspectives, you can map this visually. Where are the choke points, what are the synergies? This output gives the participants and designers a very good sense of the overlapping dependencies that need to be considered in the design of the space.

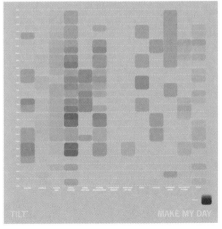

Turning over a new LeafDesk
Articulating how a space is used over the course of the day informs the choice of furniture. For our project with climate change charity 10:10 in London we created a specific iteration of our LeafDesk with seven connected leaf sections, addressing the needs of its large team. The LeafDesk is a piece of furniture that we have iterated over 20 times for different spaces, providing variations of materials, finishes and forms.

On/Off

When designing for different states, it is
important to know when certain spaces need
to have a degree of permanence. Relaxation
and quiet areas often require this. While the
dynamism of the space directly above and
behind the Hearth changes frequently, the
Hearth itself remains calm.

Object Call _____

What do our relationships to objects and each other look like when expressed spatially? More often than not a design process loses the fragile interplays of collective emotion and need. For any building to work, and for those who use it to appreciate it, we need to explore and map the tacit bonds of objects and each other.

Who said what
When creating the output for the Object Call activity, it is necessary to try to capture everything said by each participant about their object. This can be done by video or audio. The output forms part of the evolving narrative of the space.

Every object has a story
Object Call has the unique ability to engage participants on both an emotional and a practical level. When we ran this activity for a coworking space in Syracuse, Italy, we were overwhelmed by the depth of feeling people expressed through their objects. One participant brought an image of his unborn baby and placed it the space, underlining how important it was for him that the space could accommodate his new arrival.

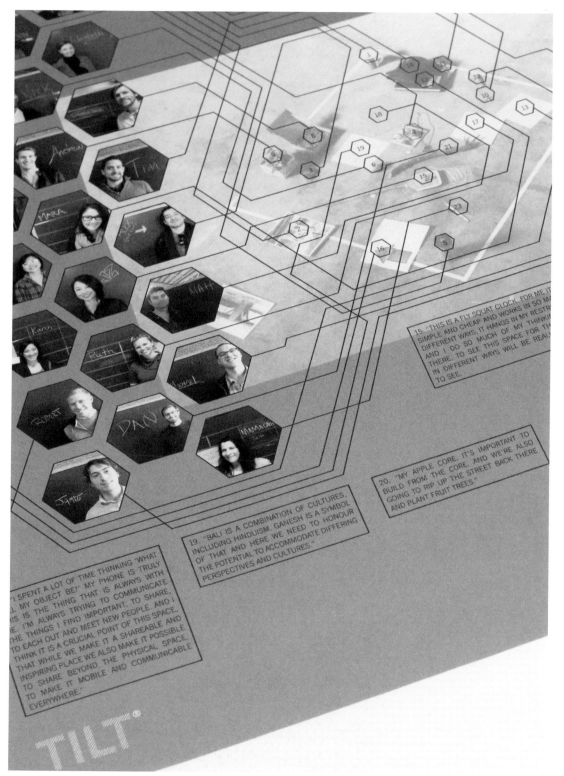

15. "THIS IS A FLY SQUAT CLOCK. FOR ME IT'S
SIMPLE AND CHEAP AND WORKS IN SO MA...
DIFFERENT WAYS, IT HANGS IN MY RESTR...
AND I DO SO MUCH OF MY THINKIN...
THERE. TO SEE THIS SPACE FOR TH...
IN DIFFERENT WAYS WILL BE REALL...
TO SEE."

20. "MY APPLE CORE, IT'S IMPORTANT TO
BUILD FROM THE CORE, AND WE'RE ALSO
GOING TO RIP UP THE STREET BACK THERE
AND PLANT FRUIT TREES."

19. "BALI IS A COMBINATION OF CULTURES,
INCLUDING HINDUISM. GANESH IS A SYMBOL
OF THAT AND HERE WE NEED TO HONOUR
THE POTENTIAL TO ACCOMMODATE DIFFERING
PERSPECTIVES AND CULTURES."

"I SPENT A LOT OF TIME THINKING 'WHAT
...L MY OBJECT 'BE?" MY PHONE IS TRULY
...IS IS THE THING THAT IS ALWAYS WITH
...E. I'M ALWAYS TRYING TO COMMUNICATE
...HE THINGS I FIND IMPORTANT, TO SHARE,
...TO EACH OUT AND MEET NEW PEOPLE. AND I
...THINK IT IS A CRUCIAL POINT OF THIS SPACE,
...THAT WHILE WE MAKE IT A SHAREABLE AND
...INSPIRING PLACE WE ALSO MAKE IT POSSIBLE
...TO SHARE BEYOND THE PHYSICAL SPACE,
...TO MAKE IT MOBILE AND COMMUNICABLE
...EVERYWHERE."

TILT®

Made in Italy
The collection of objects pictured here came from the workshop we
ran in Syracuse, Italy. Great care has been taken by the participants
when placing the objects within the space, with due consideration to
how they interrelate—note the locations of the two coffee pots! One
instantly as you enter the space and another with its own dedicated
area within the space, indicating the importance of coffee on arrival
as well as a separate cafe space elsewhere in the building.

PPPP

Working on projects in the scoping stage, often without a
building or site, means we need to understand the parameters
of the project before we begin to design. We think of these
things through the point of view of People, Planet, Profit and
Place. Each elements is explored and mapped to create
insights that can create a truly cohesive building design.

New economics

The PPPP activity has particular resonance with organisations that are driven by social purpose. During our work with nef (New Economic Foundation) PPPP helped it to understand how it could develop their building in line with its principles, incorporating a community garden, learning spaces and private apartments that would promote sustainable living through their design.

Going downtown

While working with the Downtown Project in Las Vegas, we conducted a number of workshops with members of the local community in a converted church. The PPPP activity helped participants to imagine how the wider principles of sustainability and civic development could be reflected in the space itself. Some issues were particularly relevant to the Las Vegas context such as water use, solar power, cooling and transport.

Rant Roll _____

The nature of a building is complex and fraught with compromise, so it is important to provide conduit and visibility to opinion as it progresses. The Rant Roll sits in a space and unrolls as it fills up. Often the nature of insight and opinion leads to new ideas for spaces as the project emerges, the roll capturing them as the project progresses.

Scroll down
The Rant Roll activity works very well with a high number of participants. It can be left as an installation within a space and people can interact with it without facilitation. It can also lead directly to design ideas like the rolling exhibition curated in the Oxford Hub. This Rant Roll was part of a series of interventions designed by us for the Shine Unconference to encourage engagement from attendees around the themes of the conference.

Do doodle

As with Imaginary Tables, this represents another instance where the concept behind the activity has directly influenced our design for a space. The notion of having writable surfaces in a space where people can scribble what they want is related to the Rant Roll activity. The offices of climate change charity 10:10 have a lot of volunteers coming and going, so the blackboards provide an important marking post for in-space communication.

Rapid Render: Paper _____

Moving into three dimensions—from head to hands—is a key imaginative leap as a community codesign their space. Quick and dirty is good, rather than too much consideration and deliberation. Our transformative leap into an enabling space suddenly becomes real, and we begin the exciting journey that will ultimately create the space. We work with three scales of modelling, all the way up to full scale modelling and testing life-size interactions and solutions for the space.

Baby knows best
For a project with Worcester Council, we engaged tenants of a local YMCA centre to help codesign how a homeless crash pad could be incorporated into the building. The activity worked because it was both fun but also elicited important information about the ideas for the space in a very informal way.

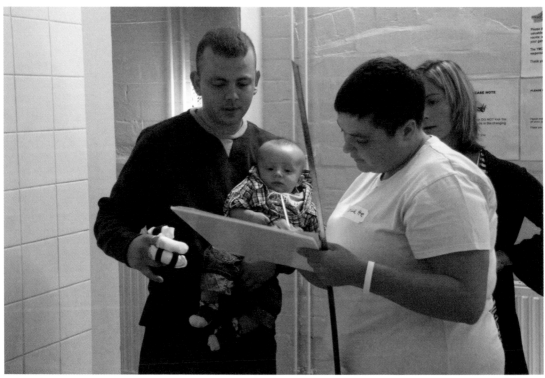

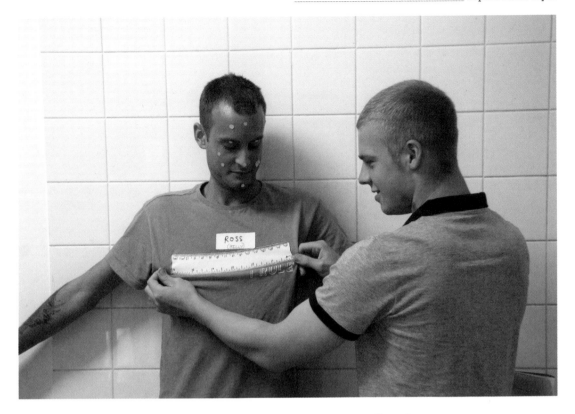

Measuring success

The true measure of a successful codesign process for us is the delivery of an effective space at the end that is fit for purpose and truly enables the user community. But there are certain intangible measures, such as the friendships that are created within the community throughout the process, that endure beyond our involvement.

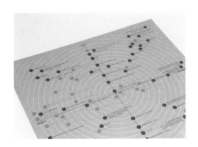

Different outputs

The series of Rapid Render activities we have developed have very different ways of being presented graphically. The paper version is about plotting listed elements as part of a scatter map of settings and attributes.

Rapid Render: Model _____

Model hospital

Our work codesigning a new Ambulatory Care Centre at the Whittington Hospital in London led us to engage staff and patients in interrogating the use of space. In the codesign workshops, participants were encouraged to develop and present models of the space. Working with playful materials helps everyone take part, removing the vulnerability often associated with so-called artistic skill.

Ambulatory zones

Mapping the interplay of zones was an extremely important exercise in the case of the Ambulatory Care Centre, since the placement of specific health services, such as paediatrics, was dependent on a number of other related factors. The staff had the appropriate knowledge, so it was crucial to engage them in the process in order to work up a cohesive zonal plan for the space.

From the smallest seed...
The shapes of the Fruit & Nut table series are inspired by natural, organic shapes. The Conker, as its name suggests, takes its shape from the conker or chestnut. We will continue to add shapes to the Fruit & Nut Series as and when ideas emerge to inspire them.

Furniture testing

Sometimes model-making is a good opportunity to test and develop furniture concepts that have emerged through the codesign process. While working with The Hub in Vienna and London, we created the Fruit & Nut Series to enable high-density working and maximise flexibility. These tables have subsequently gone on to be sold throughout the world.

Rapid Render: Full Scale _____

Cardboard cut-out

No amount of computer modelling can substitute the experience of people interacting with a mocked-up life-size version of the space. This can be done using very inexpensive materials such as cardboard and plywood. We prefer to use these types of materials because they are familiar to everyone and people are happy to get hands-on with them, work quickly and intuitively and without fear of causing damage.

Imaginary treatment room

It is a source of great frustration for us that so little time is afforded to testing healthcare environments prior to construction. For the Whittington Hospital we created a very basic prototype of a treatment room for the new Ambulatory Care Centre that allowed the health practitioners to prototype in full scale the emerging designs.

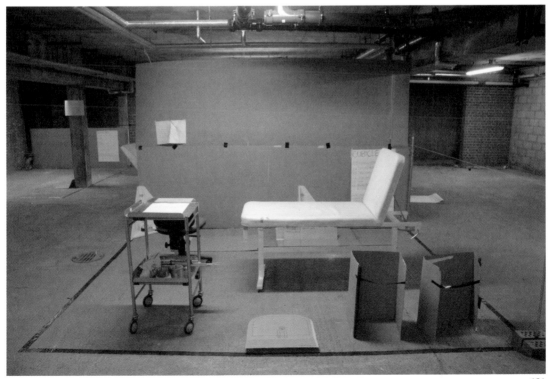

Quiet

The evolution of the Quiet can be visually traced from the basic cardboard mock-up that emerged from the codesign workshop through to the finished product. Originally conceived for our Pharmacy project at the Whittington Hospital, it has resonance in many types of space. We love the way that user needs in one specific context can be translated elsewhere.

Shrove Tuesday _____

The context of design is crucial for TILT. Lots of our activities,
at first glance, seem to have nothing to do with design.
Design happens best through the right atmosphere and setting.
Turning the act of making pancakes into an activity brings a
group together, while alluding to the historical precedent of
using things up to start something new.

Cooking at 38 Degrees
The Shrove Tuesday activity was first
introduced in a workshop with 38 Degrees,
a London-based not-for-profit organisation
focused on building online campaigns to hold
organisations to account. The activity worked
well as they were a close-knit team who
enjoyed having an opportunity to engage and
learn more about each other.

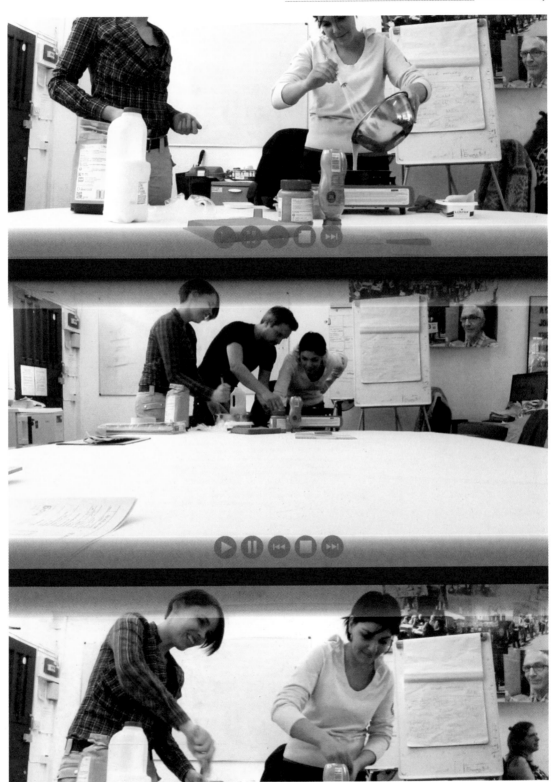

Smoke Room _____

Creating distinct experiential installations in a space to elucidate spatial perception, affinity and narratives is an essential part of codesign. Intuitive participation is essential to bring to life the relationship of the user to the physicality of the space.

Smoking permitted

When inviting people to participate in a codesign workshop, incorporating activities that challenge their sensory perception can really help to stimulate creative thinking. This activity was a big hit when we used it during the first workshop for the Student Hub project. People talked about their experience having a positive impact on others joining subsequent codesign workshops.

The Vitrine _____

Documenting process and displaying the stories that arise
from codesign helps participants to see where they've come
from in the space—what was there to be repurposed. Often
our spaces will be reused and understanding the things left
behind by others, by the previous life of the space, gives us
a way to frame and identify the present.

If walls had ears...
Every building has a unique story. Older
buildings with mixed histories, like the Student
Hub in Oxford, have particularly fascinating
stories that deserve to be told while inspiring
groups to imagine how best to create a new
identity for the space.

Reflecting the past

Sometimes it is possible to literally use part of a building's history to make its present. With the Festival Village we reused and repurposed a huge number of elements from the space. At Hub Kings Cross the collected items for the Vitrine activity found homes in the finished space.

Objectification

When presenting the Vitrine as an output, we present the objects as a curated collection which has the details of the participants' individual thoughts written beside each specific object. As participants read the stories they can get a sense of the importance of objects in respect to a space and how every piece of furniture has a role in shaping their environment.

WWWW

The 'who', 'why', 'what' and 'where' of the space. Participants work independently in groups on Imaginary Tables in the space. These questions are broad and gauge the affiliations and networks that can leverage the opportunities of the space, along with defining key concerns of the user group itself.

Why the what?

Our activities are designed to be intuitive but a designer will always introduce each activity before people engage, helping flow and understanding. We produce 'Cheet Sheets' as well, simple fold-outs that help participants assimilate in their own time how to work through the activity. The misspelling of 'cheat' is from workshops in Brazil— we like it better that way!

Seeing everything at once

When we designed see-through partition walls for Troika's office in London, it was in response to its requirement to accommodate multiple functions. Its desire to have both an informal and formal meeting room within a very small space led us to produce rooms that sat within the space but did not obscure the open-plan design of the space.

Wall flowers

Utilising all planes of a space is a key concern of our design process and one that features heavily in our finished spaces. Creating designed opportunities to store furniture, including an intuitive presentation of how to use it, while simultaneously providing an elegant visual backdrop works brilliantly here at the Festival Village.

Coworking by colour

In this coworking space we designed in London, we have used colour and furniture type to help distinguish between all the different zonal elements including touchdown and permanent working. We have also incorporated large curtains which can be used to subdivide the space as required for different functions. All of these elements help intuitive navigation of the space and maximise flexibility.

Appendix

Codesigning Space

Designing an effective structure for the book was very important for TILT. We brought together a selection of our activities, products and projects and looked again at the ways they have interacted over our practice lifetime. As a busy practice, we would never normally have the time to do this: the process of creating the book has been enlightening. This graphic demonstrates the connection between included projects and the activities used to create them, along with the products that have resulted through this work. Our products are understood through a system of prototype, open source and actual product, having put in development and resources to create a viable cost-effective item.

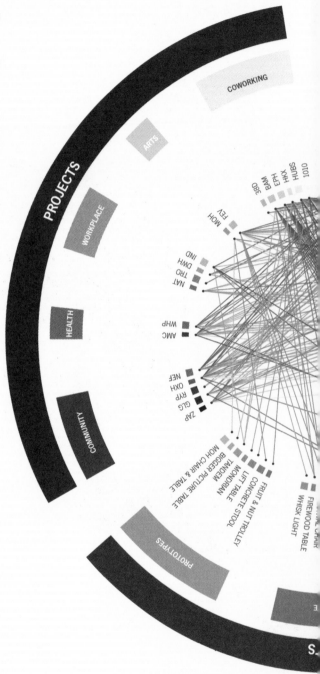

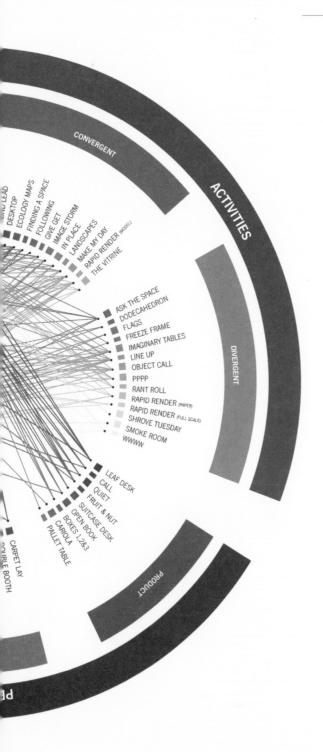

CONVERGENT

ACTIVITIES

DIVERGENT

PRODUCT

LEAD
DESKTOP
ECOLOGY MAPS
FINDING A SPACE
FOLLOWING
GIVE GET
IMAGE STORM
IN PLACE
LANDSCAPES
MAKE MY DAY
RAPID RENDER (MODEL)
THE VITRINE

ASK THE SPACE
DODECAHEDRON
FLAGS
FREEZE FRAME
IMAGINARY TABLES
LINE UP
OBJECT CALL
PPPP
RANT ROLL
RAPID RENDER (PAPER)
RAPID RENDER (FULL SCALE)
SHROVE TUESDAY
SMOKE ROOM
WWWW

LEAF DESK
CALL
QUIET
FRUIT & NUT
SUITCASE DESK
OPEN BOOK
BOXES 1,2&3
CARIOLA
PALLET TABLE

CARPET LAY
DOUBLE BOOTH

Community
ZAP Downtown Project, Las Vegas, USA
GLG Global Generation, London, England
RYP Backing Young People, Worcester, England
OXH Oxford Hub, Oxford, England
NEF New Economic Foundation, London, England

Health
AMC Ambulatory Care Centre, Whittington Hospital, London, England
WHP Whittington Hospital Outpatient Pharmacy, London, England

Workplace
NAT Natura, Manaus, Brazil
TRO Troika, London, England
DWH Devon Work Hubs, Devon, England
IND Independents United, London, England

Arts
MOH The Proud Archivist, London, England
FEV The Festival Village, London, England

Coworking
38D 38 Degrees, London, England
BAM Club Chiswick, London, England
EPH Club Bankside, London, England
HKX Hub Kings Cross, London, England
1010 10:10, London, England
HUBS including: Amsterdam, Bergen, Los Angeles, Milan, Madrid, Ottawa, São Paulo, Syracuse, Vienna and Zurich

LIST OF ILLUSTRATIONS

cover image: Hub Zurich, Zurich, Switzerland, 2010

p. 2–3: Ask the Space in action on the site of a proposed coworking space. The participants are members of the community who will be part of the new space and have an active interest in its design. The shot captures very well the dynamic flow of the activity, with people moving around freely and investigating all elements of the space. Hub Syracuse, Syracuse, Sicily, 2011

p. 9: Effective communication is and will always be an integral part of a design process. The setting for that conversation is key for a codesign process. The placing, arrangement and interaction of the participants has been considered within our design frameworks in order for an authentic and effective conversation to emerge. Hub Syracuse, Syracuse, Sicily, 2011

p. 12–13: The first in the sequence that opens each section in the book, this image is crucial for TILT. We can create, define and utilise space from nothing. The simple act of marking out a square creates the opportunity for anyone to engage, to imagine and interpret the space formed. Hub Milan, Milan, Italy, 2009

p. 14: The Festival Village explored comaking in depth. We framed building

packages that the community designed and delivered. One volunteer made the floor of the Hearth area of the space, leading a team and hand-cutting over 300 separate wooden hexagons. In one he encased a bee in resin. The bee was a symbol of the original Festival of Britain hosted on the site in the 1950s. Festival Village, London, England, 2012

p. 17: Iterative approaches to forming narrative, through iteration and experiment make sense of difficult briefs. For a project with so many stakeholders we needed to replay the ecology mapping of the space many times, looking each time at new spatial narratives. Festival Village, London, England, 2012

p. 20: We often play with spatial perception and orientation. Our lead often comes from ideas around performance and reception, giving the space new stories and meanings. Walking through the space and inviting participants to understand space non-visually is enlightening while also a significant way for people to understand how to design truly inclusive spaces. Hub Syracuse, Syracuse, Sicily, 2011

p. 24: The workshop setting is crucial to the process of codesign. It is a constructed environment from which a project's design brief can be shaped by exploring existing narratives, building new ones and investigating experiential qualities. Participants will work in groups but the role of designer, as facilitator is still key

to setting the course of the workshop and allowing it to flow. Festival Village, London, England, 2012

p. 26: The workshop stems from an instinct for gathering and debating, the need for a productive relationship between interaction with a site, its materials and its narrative to evolve meaningful design. Models in our workshop setting function as active tools to enable participants to shape, test and interrogate. Ambulatory Care Centre, London, England, 2013

p. 28: 1,000 square metres of unused space within a hospital in North London. Our projects are often renovations, and purposefully so. Reimagining space, especially in big cities, is a crucial element of the future of urban architecture. Ambulatory Care Centre, London, England, 2013

p. 31: Developing a design framework for user iteration is a crucial part of codesign. For the library at the Festival Village we worked with the programming of the Festival of the World to bring the space to life. Each poet coming to London for Poetry Parnassus, an event inviting a poet from each competing Olympic country, was asked to bring a book to be presented to the library. The library grew, along with further iterative ways to populate its shelves. Festival Village, London, England, 2012

p. 32: There is no better way of working than having everyone in the room. We face different challenges with this approach, one being how to work on bigger projects and with more participants. How can you scale the interpersonal experience of a workshop within the virtual sphere, for example, or in increasingly larger settings? Whittington Hospital Pharmacy, London, England, 2012

p. 36: Representing ideas often prompt as many questions as they can answer. But the questions are qualified and lead the project further as part of a codesign flow. Giving shape to the disparate ideas and intentions of a community through models is all part of the directed shape of codesign. Backing Young People, Worcester, England, 2012

p. 41: Alongside our codesign methodology is a parallel process of comake. It is rich and exciting in its own way and beyond the scope of this book. The Festival Village project in these pages in an example, but there are others. Challenging the paradigm of those who build and those who occupy is crucial for us and is demonstrated by this image from the comake at 10:10. Featured is our youngest ever comaker! 10:10, London, England, 2010

p. 42: Architecture is no longer distinct and needs the input of service designers, graphic designers, experience designers, technologists and the social sciences. We work in this way, putting together project teams that can transform these prototype signs, for example, into an exemplary wayfinding system. Whittington Hospital Pharmacy, London, England, 2012

p. 45: Part of the joy of codesigning is the anecdotal and emotive elements that emerge and become integral to the design solutions. While only a prototype, the wayfinding at the Whittington involved Dick's cat, a symbol of the hospital and a recognisable and loved icon. Whittington Hospital Pharmacy, London, England, 2012

p. 46: No doubt a lot of what we do has been seen before, and tried before. We're always looking towards and exploring the history of design to learn from precedent. Something feels different this time around, though. So many factors are coming together to make the work we do continuously exciting. Ambulatory Care Centre, London, England, 2013

p. 50: Having a physical series of objects to relate to is a way to accelerate spatial understanding. If those objects are created by participants it is even better, the gap between the imagination and the manifested idea suddenly is very close indeed. The expression and understanding of tacit knowledge through a process of codesign becomes accessible and effective, bringing intuitive spatial solutions to the fore very quickly. Ambulatory Care Centre, London, England, 2013

p. 52: Codesign is characterised by a multiplicity of voices. It makes room for identities to form through action and reflection. While it has become the norm for designers and architects to prescribe spaces to functions and instruct people

in what they need for their business, civic buildings, public squares, or homes, TILT has pared back the design process and begins by listening to the client and the user. Hub Syracuse, Syracuse, Sicily, 2011

p. 55: One important aspect of codesign is to combat wilful ignorance by bringing all the stakeholders of a project into the process from the start. This is the basis of codesign, a method for design rooted in an age-old appreciation of the value of inclusion. Hub LA, Los Angeles, USA, 2011

p. 56–57: A lack of tables is no barrier to participation. The simple act of getting workshop participants to create imaginary tables on the floor with tape serves to demonstrate that preconceived notions about space are often social constructs. The tables become real for purposes of the workshop and the people involved understand from the outset that they can create their own reality. Hub Milan, Milan, Italy, 2009

p. 134–135: Space is never finished. A model is being considered by a lunch crowd, taking 10 minutes away from work to consider and model layouts. The shape of their engagement, around a focus of attention, is the culmination of the three images that have introduced each section. Hub Kings Cross, London, England, 2010

CONTRIBUTORS

Tom Dyckhoff

Tom Dyckhoff is a writer and broadcaster about architecture, places and cities. He is architecture critic for BBC television's *The Culture Show*, and has presented many documentaries for British TV and radio. Tom has written a weekly column for *The Guardian* newspaper since 2000, and, from 2003 to 2011, was architecture critic at *The Times* newspaper, London. He is an Honorary Fellow of the RIBA, and trustee of the Architecture Foundation. He lives in London, with his family.

David Lan

David Lan was born in Cape Town where he trained as an actor. He moved to London and trained as a social anthropologist at the LSE. In 1985 he published a classic of modern social anthropology *Guns and Rain: Guerrillas and Spirit Mediums in Zimbabwe*. He has written many plays which have been produced by the Royal Court, the National Theatre, the RSC, the Almeida. He has travelled widely in Africa and written and directed films for BBC TV. He was appointed artistic director of the Young Vic in 2000 where he has directed and/or produced over 150 shows.

Irena Bauman

Irena Bauman is a founding director of Bauman Lyons Architects. She has also set up a CIC, 'Leeds Love it Share it' in partnership with academics and other practitioners to carry out research projects into the future needs of the city. Irena is a Professor of Sustainable Urbanism at Sheffield University School of Architecture and researches adaptation strategies to climate change. She has authored *How to be a Happy Architect* and is currently working on a book commissioned by RIBA Publishing, *Retrofitting Neighbourhoods - Designing for Resilience*

Eileen Conn MBE

Eileen Conn is a long-standing resident of Peckham, and co-ordinates Peckham Vision (www.peckhamvision.org). She worked for many years in Whitehall on the management and development of government systems. Since then she has studied social dynamics of complex living systems, and applied the results in her work for sustainable communities. She has received several awards as a community activist and in 2009 was awarded and MBE for services to the community. She is an Associate Fellow of the TSRC and is continuing the development of her social ecosystem dance model for understanding and improving community engagement.

Peter Head CBE

Peter Head is a world-renowned civil and structural engineer. He has won many awards for his work including the Award of Merit of IABSE, the Royal Academy of Engineering's Silver Medal and the Prince Philip Award for Polymers in the Service of Mankind. He led the planning and integrated urbanism team at Arup from 2004–2011. In 2008 he was named by *The Guardian* as one of 50 people that could 'save the planet' and by *Time* magazine as one of 30 global eco-heroes. In 2011 he was awarded a CBE for services to civil engineering and the environment. He established the Ecological Sequestration Trust in 2011.

Jeremy Myerson

Jeremy Myerson is the Director and Chair of the Royal College of Art's Helen Hamlyn Centre for Design. A leading author, academic and activist in the field, Jeremy developed his interest in design and innovation as a journalist and editor working on titles including *Design, Creative Review* and *World Architecture*. He was the Founding Editor of *Design Week*, the world's first weekly news magazine for designers and their clients. He has authored several books, including *New Demographics New Workspace, The 21st Century Office* and *IDEO: Masters of Innovation*. He is on the advisory boards of design schools in Hong Kong and Korea.

Mat Hunter

Mat Hunter is Chief Design Officer at the Design Council, which promotes design for the public good. Mat heads up the organisation's Design Challenges programme which demonstrates how design can drive innovation through tackling the big issues of our time, such as reducing crime or promoting health and wellness for an ageing population. Before joining the Design Council, Mat was a partner at IDEO, an internationally renowned design and innovation consultancy, where he focused mostly on creating new digital products and services. His current academic roles include Adjunct Professor at Imperial College Business School and External Examiner for Product Design at Glasgow School of Art.

THE TILT TEAM

Dermot Egan, Cofounder & Managing Director

Originally from Ireland, Dermot moved to London to complete a Master's Degree in Social and Organisational Psychology at the LSE. Prior to establishing TILT, Dermot led a UK government research project on sustainable business at Cambridge University before leaving to cofound The Hub Kings Cross in 2008. The Hub Kings Cross is part of a global network of coworking spaces providing entrepreneurs and innovators with a place to work, connect and scale their ideas. It has attracted over 800 members and supported over 200 new ventures. Dermot was named one of the 'Future 100' young entrepreneurs in 2008 and has written regular blogs for *The Guardian* on social business.

Oliver Marlow, Cofounder & Creative Director

Oliver Marlow is a multiplatform designer. With his unique skillset as a designer, craftsman, academic and facilitator, he works on all levels of the design process. Prior to founding TILT, Oliver was Head of Design at The Hub, a global network of coworking spaces. There he led the design process for over 25 Hub spaces globally. He has designed with, amongst others, Southbank Centre, the Young Vic Theatre, the Battersea Arts Centre, Edinburgh Film Festival and NPI, Shanghai, the first social innovation centre in China. He is a leading expert on the design of collaborative spaces and lectures extensively on the subject.

Tomasz Romaniewicz, Architectural Design

After graduating from Leeds School of Architecture with first class honours, Tomasz worked with PTE Architects, RIBA Building Futures, DSDHA and as an Exhibition Designer. During Postgraduate studies at the London Metropolitan University, his thesis explored an architecture hybrid with popular culture, *genius loci* and the concerns of the twenty-first century city. Tomasz has experience in the design and realisation of award-winning buildings, notably Tidemill Academy, and is currently leading projects that challenge mainstream preconceptions of workspace and the reuse of existing buildings.

Matthew Wood, Architectural Design

Matthew graduated with BA(hons) and BArch from Manchester School of Architecture. In practice, Matthew has worked on several high-profile buildings and taken a lead role in the design of award-winning private residences and public buildings. Combining his education with several years working on site, Matthew has developed a skillset which continues to be enhanced at TILT. He recently returned from working in India, where he was able to expand on an interest in social welfare, education and sustainability.

Elena Nunziata, Product Design

Born in Rome, Italy, Elena Nunziata is a furniture and product designer who started her career in arts and crafts. After exploring ceramics, painting and sculpture, she moved into design, achieving a BA in Industrial Design. She moved to London and obtained an MA in Furniture Design at Central Saint Martins College of Art and Design. Her work focuses on creative and playful exploration of design with an innate passion for interactive environments and furniture. At TILT she leads the development of new furniture design.

Ben Kindler, Graphic Design

Ben Kindler is a graphic designer born and based in London. Before turning to design, he trained and specialised in drug and alcohol misuse work for young people. During this time he started to collaborate with young people to produce publications and events. It was these initial projects that sparked his drive towards codesign and working with the target audience. As the lead graphic designer for TILT he specialises in branding, data visualisation, wayfinding and signage.

With thanks to those who have worked with TILT:

Matteo Balza, Olwen Cullen, Arianna de Luca, Vicky Jiang, Katja Knecht, Rob Leechmere, Annabel Maguire, Ganga Morton, James Moruzzi, Alastair MacKenzie, Natasha Piper, Rachel Postlethwaite, Angela Ponzini, Brad Rose and Jesson Yip. In particular, Laura Guedes and Kate Jose, who were crucial in the formative years of the practice.

COLLABORATORS

Jennifer Magnolfi

Jennifer Magnolfi is a recognised R&D consultant in the field of networked environments, high-tech workspaces, start-up spaces and coworking. In 2012 she lead the coworking development initiative for Downtown Project LLC, an investment fund by Zappos.com CEO Tony Hsieh driving the revitalisation of Downtown Las Vegas. Previously at Herman Miller, she led applied research on the effects of information technology in space. She is the co-author of *Always Building: the Programmable Environment*, articulating

the technology drivers and design principles for user-based programmability in future commercial interiors.

Andrew Lock

Andrew Lock has worked in the theatre, exhibition and architecture sectors for over 10 years. His clients include Southbank Centre, the British Library and the Barbican Centre. Andrew worked in theatre design before working with architecture and design practices and setting up his own company. He specialises in bringing his understanding of the arts to the built environment, with projects ranging from working with Sir Peter Hall to design the interior of the Rose Theatre in Kingston to creating interactive environments with leading children's theatre company Theatre-Rites, to winning a RIBA competition to design a mobile performance and event venue.

Bruno Taylor

Bruno Taylor is a designer and social entrepreneur with a strong background in service design, user insights and social innovation. He brings a user-centred design approach when taking new services and products to market. He co-founded commonground, a design consultancy working with public and third sector organisations; and Flip Yourself, a digital software company. Bruno set up the first service design course at Central Saint Martins College of Art and Design. TILT collaborated with Bruno on the Backing Young People project.

Gwen Webber

Gwen Webber is an architecture and design writer and editor. She has been based in New York as *Blueprint*'s US Correspondent, and as a contributor to *AR* and *The Architect's Newspaper*, among others. Gwen is on the Programme Committee for arts organisation, INCCA-NA and is director of a women in architecture interview project. She has also helped deliver the London Festival of Architecture and the London Design Festival. For this book, Gwen collaborated with TILT on the concept, writing and editing.

Pablo Handl

Pablo was born in Buenos Aires and grew up in Vienna. He studied business, theatre pedagogics and conflict mediation. While living and working both in India and Netherlands he was dedicated to Youth Leadership Development, serving as Director for AIESEC International in 2003. In 2006 he cofounded The HUB São Paulo and he continues to aid the development of The Hub in Brazil. Pablo led the codesign work with Natura in Manaus in collaboration with TILT.

FURTHER READING

Suggestions from the TILT team
Eisenman, Peter, *Eisenman Inside Out: Selected Writings 1963-1988* (2004) (Tomasz)

Kester, Grant, *Conversation Pieces: Community and Communication in Modern Art* (2004)
(Oliver)

Munari, Bruno, *Design as Art* (1966)
(Elena)

Sennett, Richard, *The Craftsman* (2008)
(Matthew)

Shaughnessy, Adrian, *How to be a Graphic Designer Without Losing Your Soul* (2005)
(Ben)

Surowiecki, James, *The Wisdom of Crowds: Why the Many Are Smarter Than the Few and How Collective Wisdom Shapes Business, Economies, Societies and Nations* (2005)
(Dermot)

ACKNOWLEDGEMENTS

Books and publications referenced in this book:

Victor Papanek, *Design for the Real World* (1974)
Allan Kaprow, *Art Which Can't Be Art* (1986)
Lina Bo Bardi, *Lina Bo Bardi* (1996)
John Dewey, *Art as Experience* (1934)
Henri Lefebvre, *The Production of Space* (English translation 1991)
Susan Cain, *Quiet: The Power of Introverts*

in a World That Can't Stop Talking (2012)
Jurgen Habermas, *The Structural Transformation of the Public Sphere* (1991)
Stuart Kauffman, *Investigations* (2002)
Roger Martin, *The Design of Business* (2009)
Jacqueline Vischer, *Workspace Strategies: Environment As a Tool for Work* (Dec 21, 1995)
Lucy Lippard, *Six Years: The Dematerialization of the Art Object* (1973)
Jean Francois Lyotard, *The Differend: Phrases in Dispute* (English Translation 1988)

Web links:

Urban Task Force under the chairmanship of Lord Rogers, http://www.urbantaskforce.org/UTF_final_report.pdf

Juhani Pallasmaa, http://goo.gl/GaT1gz

Community Engagement in the Social Eco-System Dance' on the TSRC, http://www.tsrc.ac.uk/Research/BelowtheRadarBtR/

With thanks to a selection of our clients
10:10 (Ben Evans, Eugenie Harvey, Cian O'Donovan, Daniel Vockins), 38 Degrees (David Babbs, Fiona Duggan), Devon Work Hubs (Rebecca Bond, Tom Dixon, Rachel Mildon, Steve Turner), Futerra (Ed Gillespie, Solitaire Townsend), Global Generation (Jane Riddiford, Nicole Van den Eijnde), Independents United (Frank Lampen, Shilen Patel, Nick Roe), Islington Council (Paul Savage, David Wright), Natura (Iguatemi Costa), New Economics Foundation (Corrina Cordon, Stewart Wallis), Southbank Centre (Natalie Highwood, Shan Maclennan), Student Hubs (Adam O'Boyle), The Hub (Amsterdam, Bergen, London, Los Angeles, Milan, Madrid, Ottawa, Porto, São Paulo, Syracuse, Vienna, Zurich), Troika (Conor McCaughan), Wallonia Coworking (Lisa Lombardi), Whittington Hospital (Sarah Davies, Helen Taylor), Worcestershire County Council (Nicola North), Workspace & Club Workspace (James Friedenthal, Alan Grant, Andrea Kolokasi, Chris Pieroni).

And a final special thanks to all those who have participated in all the codesign and comake workshops that we have run throughout our projects. While you are too numerous to mention, your willingness to participate and the strength and value of your contributions are what validate our efforts to proliferate the practice of codesigning space.

All photography by Ben Kindler, Georgina Cranston, Jill Tate, Jonny Donovan, Manon Xhaard, Oliver Marlow, Patrick Quayle, Rod Farry, Sandra Ciampone and Filippo Podesta.

Oliver would like to dedicate this book to Chloe, who always said work with people. And to Pam and Robin, with love.

Dermot would like to dedicate this book to his parents, Derry and Noreen, for their ongoing love and support.

Colophon

© 2013 Artifice books on architecture, the
architects and the authors. All rights reserved.

Artifice books on architecture
10A Acton Street
London
WC1X 9NG

t. +44 (0)207 713 5097
f. +44 (0)207 713 8682
sales@artificebooksonline.com
www.artificebooksonline.com

All opinions expressed within this publication
are those of the authors and not necessarily
of the publisher.

Designed by Amy Cooper-Wright at Artifice books
on architecture.

British Library Cataloguing-in-Publication Data.
A CIP record for this book is available from the
British Library.

ISBN 978 1 908967 35 0

No part of this publication may be reproduced,
stored in a retrieval system, or transmitted, in
any form or by any means, electronic, mechanical,
photocopying, recording, or otherwise, without
prior permission of the publisher.

Every effort has been made to trace the copyright
holders, but if any have been inadvertently
overlooked the necessary arrangements will be
made at the first opportunity.

Artifice books on architecture is an environmentally
responsible company. CoDesigning Space: A Primer
is printed on sustainably sourced paper.